WHY REVIVAL STILL TARRIES

CHAD TAYLOR

Destiny Image® Publishers, Inc.
P.O. Box 310
Shippensburg, PA 17257-0310

"Speaking to the Purposes of God for This Generation
and for the Generations to Come"

ISBN 0-7684-2275-2

For Worldwide Distribution
Printed in the U.S.A.

This book and all other Destiny Image, Revival Press,
MercyPlace, Fresh Bread, Destiny Image Fiction,
and Treasure House books are available at
Christian bookstores and distributors worldwide.

1 2 3 4 5 6 7 8 9 10 / 10 09 08 07 06 05

Call toll-free **1-800-722-6774**.
For more information on foreign distributors, call **717-532-3040**.
Or reach us on the Internet:
www.destinyimage.com

ENDORSEMENTS

"Chad has captured God's passionate heart for the lost in this book. Follow him from the pages of the Bible out into the streets of your own hometown and become the living 'letter…, known and read by all men' (2 Cor. 3:2 [NAS]) to those around you. This book will inspire you to become creative in your proclamation of the good news so that God's banqueting table will be full. It's harvest time!!!"

—Wesley and Stacey Campbell
Founding Pastors, New Life Church, Kelowna, BC
Founders: Praying the Bible International and Revival Now! Ministries

"The book *Why Revival Still Tarries* is anchored in the Word of God and given to us by a man of God, Chad Taylor, who is in the harvest fields today ministering Jesus to a lost and needy world. This blend makes for a powerful, life-changing book. As Chad points to Jesus and the fields ripe to harvest, you will be blessed, empowered, and—I pray—baptized with fire to reach this world for Christ. I encourage you to read this book now!"

—Arthur Blessitt
the man who carries the cross around the world

"Chad Taylor is the real deal. His book, *Why Revival Still Tarries*, is a 'God-time' book that carries an anointing and impartation of power evangelism that will help bring in the Great Harvest. I recommend it highly!"

—*Che Ahn*
Senior Pastor, Harvest Rock Church, Pasadena, CA

"Chad Taylor's book is a timely tool in a world on the brink of destruction and without any hope. His words are an inspiration for me to continue to labor for the Master from the dawn to setting sun. I thank Chad for making the time to challenge all of us on the front lines to go a step farther behind enemy lines to reach the lost at any cost. '*No* greater love hath a man than to lay down his life for another.' Great book."

—*Pastor Phil Aguilar*
Founder of Set Free World Wide Ministries
and pioneer of the Los Angeles Dream Center

"*Why Revival Still Tarries* is a timely message for the Church. The harvest fields are waiting. Souls are desperately crying out for answers in days of turmoil and darkness. The Church has the keys to open the doors of destiny for them, but...we must go...we cannot remain in our comfort zones within the confines of our church buildings and programs! *Why Revival Still Tarries* will provoke you...to go!"

—*Patricia King*
Extreme Prophetic

"Chad Taylor is a burning, fiery lamp in the wilderness of today's religious systems. He's a prophetic voice, awakening the hearts of men and women into passion and zeal for the lost. The heartbeat of a revivalist echoes throughout the pages of this book as he challenges all of us with a fervent call to prophetic evangelism! He ardently urges the Church to invade the marketplace with signs and wonders following. Evoking memories of Leonard Ravenhill, he cuts through tradition, stirring an unquenchable fire for the harvest. If you don't have a heart for evangelizing the lost, you *will* when you finish this book!"

—*Jill Austin*
President, Master Potter Ministries

CONTENTS

INTRODUCTION

As I sit here at this personal crossroads of my own life, the words of Paul seem crystallized in my spirit, "To me, who am less than the least of all the saints, this grace was given, that I should preach among the Gentiles the unsearchable riches of Christ" (Eph. 3:8). As I write this introduction, the images of my past seem only to underwrite the mandate and message of revival that have been burned in my heart over these often tumultuous years. I escaped from a juvenile detention home as a teen, was dramatically saved shortly afterward at the age of 17, then later, during three years in my early 20s, I was backslidden and desperate as I cried out to God again from a prison cell. These memories now only serve at the table of this message, *Why Revival Still Tarries*.

In my youth I dreamed that I could never fail. I was indestructible in all of my zeal and innocence. I truly believed that somehow the grace of God would give me a spiritual buoyancy that would never allow me to sink. Then the Lord spoke to me from the depths of my decadence in a dark moment of the soul, "Son, let me show you a road less traveled; let me show you the depth of My grace, and then—and only then—can you reveal to My people the spirit of revival that I long to pour out on them." I could not fathom in those early years that a broken and contrite heart God would not despise. I thought in my ignorance that I would never fall. If I prayed enough and fasted enough, somehow I would be immune to my own humanity. Then, from a maximum security prison cell in 1994, I cried out to God as my predecessors before me did—David, Peter, and Jonah—saying, "Lord, have mercy upon me a sinner; create in me a clean heart; renew a right spirit in me; and give back to me the joy of my salvation."

Revival still tarries because we are afraid to allow the Holy Spirit to sound out the depths of His grace in us. We are terrified of our own human frailty and we dress it up in our "Sunday best" hoping God and man will accept us. We have not understood the mystery of mercy that provoked Paul to pen these words, "But by the grace of God I am what I am" (1 Cor. 15:10, NIV). It wasn't the things Paul could do but the things he could not do that made him great. He understood his own weakness, and Christ's strength was perfected in it. Today, the jury of religion holds its stones of judgment because it is unwilling to accept its weaknesses and shortcomings. Religion drags revival to the feet of Jesus and cries out, "Teacher, this woman was caught in adultery, in the very act. Now Moses, in the law, commanded us that such should be stoned. But what do You say?" (John 8:4-5)

Revival still tarries because we have not recognized the vessels by which it comes. Revival is a perpetual experience, not a definition. It cannot be germinated in a test tube of theology; it can only be demonstrated by the radical obedience of those who pursue it. It deals with people, not statistics.

Revival still tarries because we have not known where to look for it, nor do we know the timing by which it waits. Revival is not a hand on a clock waiting for the alarm to sound. It's the bleeding, beating heart of every person who contains the treasure of eternal life—that hope of glory, Christ in us. Once we step from the porches of tradition into the ghetto of the impossible, we will begin to drink from the cup of revival. Revival is not something confined and measured and grown in air-conditioned buildings. She is waiting for us on the streets...hiding from us in nursing homes and prisons...calling to us from foreign fields and obscure places. It's a person who will approach the throne of grace with boldness and expect a miracle, who will stand on a street corner and wait for its shadow to pass by like Moses did in Israel's exodus. It's through our hands that He desires to demonstrate His glory. It's through our lips that He longs to express His personality. *We are revival!*

Why does revival still tarry? Because God's people still tarry. We have not left the catacombs of complacency and entered the battlefield of humanity. We linger in the conference lines and meeting halls hoping the Lord will "touch us" one more time. It's not a touch of casualness that God longs to give us but a taste of His fire. We need a baptism, not of water or of wine, but of the fire of God. We have been intoxicated with conferences and Christian gatherings; now, our only recourse is to escape the maze of meetings and begin to invade the marketplace. God is looking for those who will come to the awesome altar of sacrifice and leave their life there. That is the problem—we are still alive and striving to succeed when the Lord simply wants us to die. It is hard to be "crucified with Christ" when living is our best friend.

Why does revival still tarry? Because our hearts are yet unbroken. Our pride and dignity are still intact. When we see the tear-stained faces of religion's orphans we can still walk by untouched and without emotion. When Jesus saw them He wept. When Jesus was confronted by their poverty and sin He healed them. He left the favor of the 99 for the shame of the 1. His was a life of lack but more love; ours is a life of excessive prosperity but no power. We have no revival because we have not wanted one. Oh, we have prayed feverishly for one, but we have not lived as if we wanted one. Revival is not a program; it is a person. It's the moment you reach out beyond the tapestries and trappings of contemporary Christianity into the broken heart of your neighbor. The warm insulation of modern church has created a chasm of tradition that the lost dare not cross. Rather than bridge that gap we have only emphasized it by our traditions and left behind the wreckage of a generation. Jesus said it better, "Thus have ye made the commandment of God of none effect by your tradition" (Matt. 15:6, KJV).

Why does revival still tarry? Because we have let the fire of it pass us by. We are still standing at the depot of empty experiences with our religious baggage, and the train of revival has already gone. When Jesus looked over Jerusalem and wept, He cried out, "If you had known, even you, especially in this your day, the things that make for your peace! But now they are hidden from your eyes" (Luke 19:42-44). Revival had come to Jerusalem in the form of their Messiah, and they never saw it. Their destruction—as Jesus predicted—only came because they failed to discern the "day of their visitation." We have had a "day of visitation" for 300 years in America and, by and large, we have ignored it. Revival has been waiting for us on every street corner, every marketplace, and every dark backdrop of American experience, but we have passed her by on our way to the next meeting.

Revival still tarries because it is no longer our highest pursuit. We have chased everything but it. We have been unwilling to pay the price that revival still demands. Revival cannot be scheduled or dictated in a day planner; it will interrupt and disorganize everything. It turns over the tables of pre-planning and leaves you with divine chaos. It upsets and offends. It reminds us who is really in control of our lives—God. It tears off the roof of religious structure and lowers the sick in. It stops the parade of spiritual plagiarism and cries out, "Jesus, Son of David, have mercy on me!" It ruins self-effort, leaves our hands empty of striving, and fills our heart with the rarefied boldness of divine inspiration. It cannot be managed or manipulated but simply received as we embrace the sacrificial lifestyle that it requires— less of me and more of Him. "He must increase, but I must decrease" (John the Baptist, John 3:30).

Why does revival still tarry? Because we have learned to live without it. By far this is the most dire dilemma of them all. We have grown so accustomed and conditioned to living within a passive state rather than a passionate one that we have become satisfied and content with the lesser. We live from Sunday to Sunday or meeting to meeting, and our entire Christian experience orbits around them. I dare you to peek through the keyhole of the impossible and see beyond our current conditioned rationale into a different world, a revived one where church is every day and the lost are added to it perpetually...where the intense pleasure of this holy pursuit is not rationed to us by conference speakers or church etiquette, but rather is a constant and daily adventure where the blind can see, the deaf can hear, and the lame can walk...where Samaria is saved and the uttermost parts of the earth hear our cry, "I beseech thee, shew [us] Thy glory" (Exod. 33:18, KJV). Friend, revival still tarries because we do.

A PRAYER OF REVIVAL

Lord, I see my lack. I see the emptiness of my own works. I see the dead efforts of my own hands and, like Cain, I have tried to pass them off as righteous. Forgive me. Burn up the wood, hay, and stubble of my own efforts and replace them with the refined gold of Your will. Remove far from me the rituals and routines of modern religion and burn in me Your passion for the reality of the Holy Spirit. Clean off the debris of dead works that clutters the altar of my heart and help me make a living sacrifice. Help me to give myself to You completely and utterly.

Once Your fire has touched me and consumed me, Lord, then brand my heart with Your passion—the lost and the dying.

Give me a divine revelation of what it means to take up my cross and follow You. Show me that apostolic creed, "That I may know Him, and the power of His resurrection, and the fellowship of His sufferings, being made conformable unto His death" (Phil. 3:10, KJV). Show me what it means to suffer with You and to take upon myself the same pain that You feel for people who are void of the knowledge of Your salvation. Take a sliver from Your rugged cross and put it in mine. Let me feel that holy intrusion with every breath. Show me the secret that, "If we suffer, we shall also reign with Him" (2 Tim. 2:12, KJV).

Lord, now show me how brief my time in this life is. If I can grasp that reality, then I will live every day as if it were my last one on this earth. I pray now with David, "Lord, remind me how brief my time on earth will be. Remind me that my days are numbered and that my life is fleeing away" (see Ps. 39:4). Lord, let me pour out my heart like water before Your face so that when You *do* come for me I am not fat and content, but rather empty and poured out. Let me be a drink offering to You, O Lord. Sip from the cup of my life and be satisfied. Search me and know me, O Lord, and see if there is any apathy in me that breeds indifference. Remove this far from me, O Lord, and let me be "the light of the world and a city upon a hill that cannot be hid" (see Matt. 5:14). Let me be a blazing ensign of Your life and death, Your love and passion. Let me be revived, O Lord!

CHAPTER 1

AT EASE IN ZION

Woe to you who are complacent in Zion, and to you who feel secure on Mount Samaria, you notable men of the foremost nation, to whom the people of Israel come (Amos 6:1, NIV).

The word *complacent* in Webster's Dictionary means "self-satisfied, or content, exhibiting self-satisfaction." There has never been a more descriptive and accurate definition for this present church age: "self-satisfied, content, and exhibiting self-satisfaction." Amos must have peered through the curtains of space and time and peeked into our contemporary conferences as he wrote:

*You lie on beds inlaid with ivory and lounge on your couches. You dine on choice lambs and fattened calves. You strum away on your harps like David and improvise on musical instruments. You drink wine by the bowlful and use the finest lotions, but you do not grieve over the ruin of Joseph. Therefore you will be the first to go into exile; **your feasting and lounging will end** (Amos 6:4-7, NIV).*

The name *Amos* means "burden-bearer"—which is quite appropriate since Amos carried the burden of Israel in a time of complacency and indifference. He prophesied to a people who were confident and proud of their social and spiritual standing. They were insulated from the "affliction of Joseph" and, like their forefathers before them, they reveled in the blessings as their brother lay dying in a pit. They trusted in the "Mountain of Samaria" or their positions and status quo, rather than the God of Abraham, Isaac, and Jacob. They distracted themselves with "music like David," anointed their heads with the "chief ointments," and drank the finest wines, oblivious of the pending judgment on their contentedness. They lay on beds of ivory and relaxation, enjoying only the best from their pastures and sheep while the brutal battle for souls raged around them.

In all of their exotic and exuberant worship, they had detached themselves from the ruin or affliction of their brother. Their conferences and convening created an isolation and insulation to those who were lost, perishing, and sold into slavery. Then, suddenly, in the midst of their dining and dancing, God sent a prophet, one without pedigree or title but a prophet nonetheless. His blazing message branded history with these words, "Woe to you who are complacent in Zion and to you who feel secure on Mount Samaria, you notable men of the foremost nation, to whom the people of Israel come" (Amos 6:1, NIV).

Amos' message is related intimately to us today. Never has there been a time in 2,000 years of Christianity when we have become more at ease than in the American church. In any given city of America you will find thousands of Christians with endless ads and billboards, each shouting to the world to come and visit them. Yet, in the shadow of their steeples and a stone's throw from their conferences, there are masses who are literally dying and on the razor's edge of a damnable eternity. These Christians have left the pure and undefiled religion for a self-gratifying and self-pleasing one. If I dare say, the pronouncements and judgments of Amos are relevant to this generation as well: "Therefore they shall now go captive as the first of the captives, and those who recline at banquets shall be removed" (Amos 6:7).

The church meeting is not an end-all of God's glory but only the beginning. We must begin to demonstrate this Scripture to the world, "Freely you have received, freely give" (Matt. 10:8). A careening world that is suicidal and at the ragged brink of eternity, in a great valley of decision as it fluctuates between Heaven and hell, needs more than our new CD and/or book; it needs a demonstration of Jesus Christ. Yet, at the door of most conferences is a vanguard of obstacles keeping the world out. Upon entering, people are confronted with registration tables and cash registers, leaving them with the indelible impression that salvation costs $99.99. Can't we see the message that we are conveying to a world when Jesus set the standard 2,000 years ago? "But when you give a feast, invite the poor, the maimed, the lame, the blind. And you will be blessed, because they cannot repay you; for you shall be repaid at the resurrection of the just" (Luke 14:13-14).

What happened? Where did the Church go off course? When did we become "at ease in Zion"? I believe the tide of indifference began to rise as our selfishness and desire for gifts, prophecy, and position did. We chase after titles; Amos reviled them. "Then answered Amos, and said to Amaziah, I was no prophet, neither was I a prophet's son; but I was an herdman, and a gatherer of sycomore fruit: And the Lord took me as I followed the flock, and the Lord said unto me, Go, prophesy unto My people Israel" (Amos 7:14-15, KJV). Prophets are now produced at assembly-line speed in our meetings and then sent out with a handful of tapes and books but never taught the "affliction of Joseph" or the power to be His witnesses. The best we can do is "strum away on our harps like David and improvise on musical instruments, drink wine by the bowlful and use the finest lotions while dining on choice lambs and fattened calves" (see Amos 6:4-7). Have we so soon forgotten that the fatted calf is for the prodigal and the lost?

We are about to cross the line of offense if we do not start opening the doors and exhibiting what Christ instructed us to so long ago. That we are not grieved or moved by their hurt or pain as He was is a great sin and offense to God. We do not weep as He wept over His city. In all of our conferencing and meeting, we have lost the brokenness and contriteness of Christ; in so doing, we have grieved the Holy Spirit. There is still only one dynamic that brings *more* joy in Heaven than is already there—when one soul is saved. Satan will give "all the kingdoms of this world" for one soul; how much will we give? Isn't it a tragedy, friend, when satan values souls more than we do? When hell and its hordes invest more time and energy into the streets of our cities than the Church does, we are in terrible trouble. Amos and Haggai must have somehow been related in their message. In Haggai 1:4 (NLT) the prophet asks, "Why are you living in luxurious houses while My house lies in ruins?"

When Philip had a "conference" in Samaria "there was great joy in that city" (Acts 8:8, NLT). The entire city was impacted and saved. We cannot continue to fall into the same trap that Israel did so long ago, becoming "*self-satisfied, content, and exhibiting self-satisfaction*," and expect God to bless us. On the contrary, we must be transfigured, broken, and moved by the condition of our streets and cities and do all we can to narrow the margin between the Church and the street. Incorporating the lost and the outcast into our conferences, meetings, and church services—thus satisfying the Father-heart of God—is our mandate. The Church of tomorrow will not be marked by self-seeking and self-indulgence but by a generation of passionate worshipers, soul winners who will follow in the footsteps of Christ. "For the Son of man is come to seek and to save that which was lost" (Luke 19:10, KJV). Are you one of these?

CHAPTER 2

JEREMIAH: THE
HEART OF A PROPHET

*My eyes fail with tears, my heart is troubled; my bile is poured
on the ground because of the destruction of the daughter of my
people, because the children and the infants faint in the streets
of the city* (Lamentations 2:11).

In a time of national calamity and moral collapse there was
a heart that burned with the fire of repentance and righteousness. In the midst of riot and rampage through Israel's streets
stood one lone prophet with the message of the hour mixed
with tears. Like Ramah, he refused to be comforted (see Matt.
2:18). Like his Lord, he could not ignore the plight of his people. He witnessed and pleaded on the corner of every street and
hedge of Jerusalem for their lives and their liberties; begging
them to truly return to the Lord. Echoing through the alleys and
lanes of the city his message could be heard:

Arise, cry out in the night! At the beginning of the watches;
pour out your heart like water before the presence of the Lord!
Lift up your hands toward Him for the life of your young chil-
dren, who faint from hunger at the head of every street!
(Lamentations 2:19)

Jeremiah was not a stranger to his nation's sin and pain. He did not simply observe the passing of the publican and prostitute who paraded through the streets of Jerusalem from a terraced temple treasury. He did not stand and do nothing as high priest and judge as he observed the agony and cry of Zion's children. On the contrary, he walked with them, he pleaded with them, and he wept with them! Like his Messiah, he was no stranger to their desperation; he stood with them at the threshold of their judgment and cried, "Then you will call upon Me and come pray to Me, and I will listen to you. And you will seek Me and find Me, when you search for Me with all your heart" (Jer. 29:12-13). "Now as He drew near, He saw the city and wept over it" (Jesus over Jerusalem, Luke 19:41). *Judgment should never fall without the tears of the prophet falling first.*

Yet today in modern-day clergy, hidden behind insulated church walls, one can easily stand afar off and preach of their plight, but never fight the good fight, and sleep unaware through the night and never shine His glorious light. It's easier to preach of their demise, than to look them in the eyes. It is less toil to walk by on the other side, than to bind up their wounds with oil and wine. God is looking for prophets who will weep with those who weep, leave the 99 for just 1 lost sheep and open the prison doors to set the captives free. The Lord is imploring in this dark hour, *"Who will really follow Me?"*

From the womb the stirring was heard, "Before I formed you in the womb I knew you; before you were born I sanctified you; I ordained you a prophet to the nations" (Jer. 1:5). In the bowels of the earth before the foundations of the world an election and a calling was born. It was not by mere whim or human standards that Jeremiah was ordained a prophet to the nations. Hear his reply! "Ah, Lord God! Behold, I cannot speak, for I am a youth" (Jer. 1:6). In his spiritual infancy Jeremiah fled the holy calling. In his natural age he deemed himself unfit. But in God's sovereignty he was "prophet to the nations" (Jer. 1:5).

But with no small cost did Jeremiah don this mantle! No, but with life and honor, tears and blood did he bear it. In peril and in prison did it accompany him. He was called by God to stand in the streets and weep as a nation faltered, to bear their wounds and weep their tears. In his own words he confesses, "I am the man who has seen affliction" (Lam. 3:1, NIV). Not unlike his Master and Lord he was "smitten of God, and afflicted" (Isa. 53:4, KJV).

If we desire to speak as these prophets spoke and if we aspire to live as these prophets lived, then we must enter into the melee of human despair and give the river of life freely as they did! We must step into the masses and declare with Peter, "Repent therefore and be converted!" (Acts 3:19). We can't stand afar off in some upper room writing and wrangling; we must step out of the boat of human effort and enter into the supernatural realm of His glory. You see, His power *followed* them as they went, "confirming the word with signs following" (Mark 16:20, KJV). The Lord is still looking for those whom *He* can follow.

Read this and weep, "To whom also He shewed Himself alive after *His passion* by many infallible proofs, being seen of them forty days, and speaking of the things pertaining to the kingdom of God" (Acts 1:3, KJV). The word passion comes from the Greek word *pascho* (pas'-kho), which means "to experience a sensation or impression (*usually painful*): to feel, passion, *or to suffer*, vex" (emphasis added). Jesus did not walk in divine power without *passion*, without *suffering*, and without paying the price of pain as He held an orphaned child, or healed a dying leper, or defended and forgave the prostitute. *He suffered with them! He walked with them every day! He felt their pain!* He stood in their midst. He was found with the unlovely and those deemed misfit.

My friends! This divine power does not come without passion! Nor will it ever come without His compassion! If we are to see His miracles we must first feel His heart. We must first be broken with the weight of His love before we can be equipped with the power of His glory. Today we think passion can be transferred by a spool of a tape or the ink of a book. Never! Passion can only be imparted by walking with those for whom you are passionate and by tasting the salt in the tears they cry. O Lord, give us passion!

We must leap from the safe shores of church into the deep waters of the world and take in a great catch. He's calling to us from the storm, "Don't be afraid, it is I!" He's calling us from the highways and hedges, "Compel them to come in!" He's calling us from the nations and poverty-stricken places, "The heathen is for your inheritance!" The Lord of the harvest is crying to the Church and those who stand idle, saying, "Will you work in My fields?" Jeremiah knew their pain firsthand. He sat with them every day. He pleaded and begged for their repentance. He comprehended that there was no power without passion. He knew the secret of His Father's heart: "The Lord's loving kindnesses indeed never cease. For His compassions never fail" (Lam. 3:22, NAS).

Jesus was *moved* with compassion when He saw the multitudes and from it He "heal[ed] every kind of disease and every kind of sickness" (Matt. 9:35-36, NAS). It is His compassion that will release miracles, signs, and wonders. And it is apathy and indifference that will obstruct and hinder the river of His love through earthen vessels. We expect power without passion and miracles without compassion. God forbid we live our lives without the infallible proofs of His resurrection bearing witness upon our ministry, having the power to affect the world around us that is wretched and reeling in darkness. God forbid we are silent as the world is screaming for His love, which is captured in human hearts that refuse to release it. Someone get the key of obedience and let this great love out!

"My soul, my soul! I am in anguish! Oh, my heart! My heart is pounding in me; I cannot be silent, because you have heard, O my soul, the sound of the trumpet, the alarm of war" (Jer. 4:19, NAS). Certainly from this generation is springing up an army of prophets and prophetesses...a vanguard of youth who have heard the beat of His heart and who march to its rhythm...an army that has heard in their closets the sound of the trumpet rousing the warriors to battle and are willing to follow it...a troop of youth who have counted the cost of discipleship and have plunged into the deep and cast their nets on the other side of religion—*liberty!* Certainly a *chosen generation* is taking center stage as the curtain of destiny is parting. A *royal priesthood,* who wear the stained garments of praise and humility, a *peculiar people* indeed march into the land under the banner of His love. These are the ones who will carry His glory into the nations. These are the ones who will stand before millions and declare a new day. Like Job they will exclaim, "I have heard of You by the hearing of the ears, *but now my eyes see you*" (Job 42:5, NAS).

This is a generation that not only has *heard* of His power and majesty, but one that will *experience* His power and majesty. They will *see with their eyes* the demonstration of His love and glory poured out on a dry and thirsty land. The Lord would say, "Make way! Make way for my young ones! They will lead you into the Promised Land! They will lead you into the fruitful stand! For this is a generation that finally understands the divine strategy of My unfolding plan! To possess the land! To possess the land!"

This will be a people who touch, not just talk. Like their predecessors, Jeremiah and Ezekiel, they will stand in the city gates and prophesy: " 'Return, backsliding Israel,' says the Lord;

'I will not cause My anger to fall on you. For I am merciful,' says the Lord…Only acknowledge your iniquity, that you have transgressed against the Lord your God" (Jer. 3:12-13a). They will not be foreigners, but *friends* to their nation, their city, and their land. They will stand in the gap, that God would not destroy it.

A PRAYER

God, give us prophets who are not afraid to walk in the streets with a "Thus says the Lord" message. We need people who are not afraid to touch and hold and heal the wounds of a generation, never crossing the street to the side of indifference as the priest and Levite did in the story of the Good Samaritan. Make them like their Master, who sat and ate with the publican and the tax collector despite the ridicule of His peers. Give them a courage that transcends religious tradition, which only creates a chasm between the world and Christianity instead of a bridge. God, give us Heaven-breathed, passion-born, and love-inspired prophets who invade every modern-day Samaria with Your power and eternal weight of glory, illuminating the poverty of sin with the power of Christ's liberty and breaking the chains of humanity with the promise of salvation's immortality! *GOD, GIVE US PROPHETS!*

Chapter 3

Qualifications of a Prophet

It's a common understanding that we are in a prophetic era according to the Book of Joel and later confirmed in the second chapter of Acts. It's a prophetic people who have the capacity to carry His word into a hostile and violent world and cause it to cry out, "*Men and brethren, what shall we do?*" What could possibly qualify us for such a monumental task? What could possibly give us the impact we so desperately need to change the course of cities and nations?

Look at David for a moment—a king, a psalmist, a slayer of giants, but even more important, *a man after God's own heart.* This was the qualification of Heaven that made this ruddy shepherd boy king of Israel and prophet of the Most High God. Yet in this present hour, if you read a popular prophetic book, attend a prophetic conference, say a token prayer, suddenly you're Moses overlooking rebellious Israel! The problem is that we never take the heartbreaking, soul-wrenching, mind-transforming, reputation-wrecking time with the Chief Apostle of our faith, Jesus Christ. We suddenly take upon ourselves the mantle of Elijah, never paying the price that Elijah paid.

Prophets in these days are mass-produced instead of tested and tried. Like an assembly line we produce prophets, refusing to admit that prophets are not man-made, they are God-made. They're not created in conferences and prophetic seminars, but rather in the womb, ordained by God Himself: "Before you were born I sanctified you" (Jer. 1:5). The only fingerprints that should be on the prophet's heart are God's.

First, you must make the awesome sacrifice of time, dreams, aspirations, and even life itself and sit at the Master's feet, taking on His nature and heart. Then and only then can you take on the responsibility of prophet and teacher of Israel. Let His face be the face that you first see before any man's. Let it be Heaven's mandates that rule your heart and not human persuasion or self-promotion. "Let this mind be in you which was also in Christ Jesus" (Phil. 2:5). That is the office of the prophet.

At the table with the Twelve eating their last meal together, we find an interesting scenario. In John 13:24, we see Peter asking John to inquire who will betray the Master. "He [John] then lying on Jesus' breast saith unto Him, Lord, who is it?" (John 13:25) In a room full of Jesus' closest followers, His apostles, only one knew His heart! Astounding. Yet this is no new thing. How many are leaning on His chest and hearing the rhythm of His heartbeat today? How many are feeling His breath on their face, His arm on their shoulder? Or how many have to go to the next popular conference and hear another man's version? It's one thing to be in the same room with the Lord, even in His presence, but who is close enough to whisper in His ear? Close enough to hear what He replies? God is seeking those who don't just love His presence, but love His heart and His desire—those who have taken the time to do nothing but hear Him and then respond accordingly.

We can leave wrought-up meetings, clothes disheveled from falling down in the prayer line, yet walk out into the world and make no impact. We drive the safest route home, like the priest and Levite in Jesus' parable of the Good Samaritan. We pass by many who are desperately in need of the same oil and wine that we've so carelessly received. The true prophet won't hoard the anointing from one meeting to the next. He or she will become a conduit of holy love to a dying world. Is this asking too much?

Are you a person after God's own heart? You can be. John was not preferred above the rest of the disciples; he only took the time to be close to the Master. The same invitation is to all of us, right now, even where you sit. Lean on His breast and hear His deepest thoughts. Hear the rhythm of His heart. His longing and cry is still, "What, could you not watch with Me one hour?" In all of our business in life and ministry, let's not be Martha, but rather Mary, sitting at His feet, listening to the Master's voice. Let's be the lovers of the Lord, not just His followers.

In a world riddled with contempt for life and a hatred for what's right, reckless in its pursuit of pleasure and strife, there's another aspect of the prophetic that plays a critical if not defining role in this hour: the power to create unity and true love in the Body of Christ. Let's look at the discourse in First Samuel 18:1 (KJV): "And it came to pass, when he [David] had made an end of speaking to Saul, that the soul of Jonathan was knit with the soul of David, *and Jonathan loved him as his own soul.*"

When the prophet speaks, it causes a knitting in the spirit to take place. It causes a spontaneous increase in love and compassion in the hearts of God's people for one another. It's this kind of love that will be the overcoming factor in the days ahead. It was this kind of love that saved David's life from the wrath of Saul. It's this kind of love that will be the survival of the Church in the perilous times to come. This is the foremost task of the prophet, or a prophetic people, "But speaking the truth in love, may grow up into Him in all things, which is the head, even

Christ" (Eph. 4:15, KJV). It's a call of love, a project of passion. Nothing less will get the job done, for it "...maketh *increase* of the body unto the edifying of itself in love" (Eph. 4:16, KJV).

In First Samuel 18:4 (KJV), we find another act of prophetic love unfolding: "And Jonathan stripped himself of the robe that was upon him, and gave it to David, and his garments, even to his sword, and to his bow, and to his girdle." There was covenant love and covenant commitment in the hearts of these two young men. They *loved* each other like men of God should. There wasn't a competitive bone in their bodies; their love was unto death. This kind of love will be the proof of the prophetic and apostolic order that the Lord is establishing in the earth today—a love that knows no boundaries or limitations in its giving and sacrifice for one another in the light of God's presence. It's this kind of love that will change nations and topple principalities and powers. David needed Jonathan, and Jonathan needed David. We can't do it alone.

Now we see another drama of love playing itself out in John 13:4: "[Jesus] rose from supper and laid aside His garments, took a towel and girded Himself." This was not the last time the Master would be stripped and left naked because of His love for mankind. Not too long from this time of washing, He would find Himself stripped of His garments again and hung on a cross, but this time the washing would be by His blood. "If I then your Lord and Teacher, have washed your feet, you also ought to wash one another's feet" (John 13:14). This is the life of the servant of Jesus Christ. It's one of unselfish giving and pouring one's self out. So we see a picture of the prophet and a clear portrait of the apostle characterized by selfless love and sacrifice: that "nothing be done in strife or vainglory, but in lowliness of mind let each esteem other better than themselves.... Let this mind be in you, which was also in Christ Jesus" (Phil. 2:3,5, KJV).

This is the holy standard of love that has been passed down to us through the centuries. No less than this can affect a world covered in gross darkness; no less than this can pierce this darkness and translate the lost into the Kingdom of His dear Son. It must be our highest mark that we strive for, "the prize of the high calling of God in Christ Jesus" (Phil. 3:14, KJV).

Church! It's time to lay down our crowns and our reputations and with Paul cry to the Lord: "But what things were gain to me, these I counted loss for Christ" (Phil. 3:7). Let's strip off the armor of our own success, lay it at our brother's feet, and enter a prophetic covenant relationship with one another in Christ Jesus. Let's be a Barnabas, giving our land and houses and laying our trophies down, stripping off the garments of self-adorning and donning the towel of humility and sacrifice, and wash away the sin we see in others with the water of pure love. Through these acts the entire world will know that we are who we say we are—Christians (see Phil. 4:7).

Are you a prophet? Then you'll lay down your life for the brethren. You will have no hidden agenda for self, only Christ. You will never seek your own glory, only His. Your heart will be broken for the lost and dying. Why? Because His is. And as He was in the world, so will you be. You will prefer the success of others before your own. You will leap for joy when others cast out your name as evil and separate you from their company for the Lord's sake. You will not complain, only praise. You will not be a herald of doom only, but hope—hope in a God who loves the world more than life itself and paid for it with His own blood. Can you do any less? "...Because He laid down His life for us. And we also ought to lay down our lives for the brethren" (1 John 3:16, KJV). These are the undeniable marks of a servant of the Most High God; without them you are not what you say you are—a prophet.

Once a man said to me, "Chad, I can't go down to the streets like you do. I'm a prophet, not an evangelist. I've led only one person to the Lord all my life." What a lack of understanding we have of the prophetic ministry! Jesus the Chief Apostle made it His passion to save those who are lost, and said to those He had called into ministry, "As the Father has sent Me, so send I you" (John 20:21). It's not the evangelist alone who's commissioned to preach the gospel. It's every soul who has the substance of Jesus abiding in it. We are all called to be His witnesses.

In Acts 1:8 we see a power point of the Christian life. The verse states that when the Holy Spirit comes upon us, *we will receive power to be Christ's witnesses!* This is the power to testify of the resurrection and life of Jesus Christ. This was the consummation of all the apostles taught: "For I delivered to you first of all that which I also received: that Christ died for our sins according to the Scriptures, and that He was buried, and that He rose again the third day according to the Scriptures" (1 Cor. 15:3-4). It was for this very same message that nearly all of them were martyred. The sure sign of the baptism of the Holy Spirit is not only speaking in other tongues; it's the power to save a soul. Have you saved one today?

The cry of the Father's heart is the cry for a lost and desperate world. It's the statement of Peter that best defines the heart of God in this hour. "The Lord is not slack concerning His promise, as some count slackness, but is longsuffering toward us, not willing that any should perish but that all should come to repentance" (2 Pet. 3:9).

Now we know what the will of the Lord is for our lives! First, we know what it isn't! "Not willing that any should perish." Then we know what it is! "But that all should come to repentance." How does that happen? "Go therefore and make disciples of all the nations, baptizing them in the name of the Father and of the Son and of the Holy Spirit, teaching them to observe all things that I have commanded you; and lo, I am with you always, even to the end of the age" (Matt. 28:19-20).

It happens when each of us comprehends with all the saints, what's the width and length and depth and height, to *know* the love of Christ that passes knowledge, that you may be filled with all the fullness of God (see Eph. 3:16-20). When we *know* the love of the Father for His world, we will finally grasp the magnitude of our calling while on this earth and work with all abandonment to see it fulfilled. "Therefore pray the Lord of the harvest to send out laborers into His harvest" (Matt. 9:38).

CHAPTER 4

PREPARING

FOR HARVEST

*This people says, "The time has **not** come, the time that the Lord's house should be built"* (Haggai 1:2).

In an hour of gross darkness and impending change, the popular opinion is one of ease and relaxation. A state of casualness permeates the air, and somehow the plea of help that rings in the streets of America is ignored. The casual Christian meanders by the masses, oblivious to their eternal plight of doom. We shift our eyes from their blank faces and the startling images that remind us of a dying, crucified Jesus who paid a terrible price for these lives that we can so easily become deaf and dumb to. A landslide opinion says, "Everything's ok! No need to be alarmed! Everything is as it was!" The words of Peter are overlooked: "But the end of all things is at hand: be ye therefore sober, and watch unto prayer" (1 Pet. 4:7, KJV). We have declared in our casualness, "The time *has not* come, the time that the

Lord's house should be built!" What's the Lord's reply to His Church in this hour? "Consider your ways" (Hag. 1:5, KJV).

A state of transition grips the Church. The old and familiar ways do not satisfy the people. The hunger of the believer will no longer tolerate the old manna, the old tradition. There's a cry for the Living Bread, the Bread that comes from Heaven! There's a thirst for the Water that will eternally quench the spiritual palate and leave us giving more. This is the cry from the corridors of church: "MORE! Give us more! More of Your power and love so that I can effectively walk out into the marketplaces of my city and have them exclaim, 'What must I do to be saved?' Lord, we must have enough of You to pour out to the poor and hungry who stare at us from the street corner, forlorn and forgotten, and to have a place that will take them in and heal their hearts and bind up their wounds and set them free. Give us more of the power of God to cast out demons, heal the sick, and raise the dead! Give us more of this power to trample on serpents and scorpions and set our cities and streets free from the hold of darkness and sin. Yes! Give us this! Give us Him and only Him!"

The transition that grips the Church in this hour is from one of preaching to training. A simple dialogue of revelation is no longer sufficient. We must train believers for works of ministry, equipping instead of entertaining. We must "commit these things to faithful men that they can teach others also" (see 2 Tim. 2:2). We must demonstrate to them how to effectively transform their neighborhoods from ghettos to refuges where the children can safely walk. This will demand that we take the price tags off of our services and our conferences, that we accommodate the poor and dying instead of the rich and famous. Only then will we experience a national awakening and the fullness of God's blessing.

The call to leaders in this hour is to prepare the Church for harvest. For the Church to have the knowledge and ability to save a soul, to lay hands on a sick person and see him healed, to confront a gang member with the gospel message and see him converted, its people must be trained. This is the mandate from Heaven, "Prepare My people for harvest. Prepare My people for the great catch that's coming upon the Church." We can't delay in this heavenly mandate! *We must prepare the Church for harvest.* In the '70s the Church made a grave error; it failed to accommodate the youth and the historical move of God that was on their heels. God is giving the Church a second chance to influence an entire generation and its sub-cultures. We need to be facilitators of revival, not just orators of it. We must suffer the little children to come unto Him... (see Mark 10:14).

The transition is to facilitate His glory and the imminent influx into the Kingdom of God. If we will lift up our eyes, we will see a sea of souls beckoning laborers into fields that are white and heavy with fruit. The ripe fields sway in the winds of His Spirit, who woos them and draws them to the cross and Christ. We must be ready to receive them. This is the anointing that's upon us: "...to preach good news to the poor...to proclaim freedom for the prisoners and recovery of sight for the blind, to release the oppressed..." (Luke 4:18, NIV).

This is the generation that will capture the favor of the Lord. This is the generation that will arrest His enemies with a glory unprecedented. This is the time to prepare the nets, repair the riggings and boats, launch out into the deep, and take in a great catch. This is the heart of the Father; this is the heart of His Son; this is the heart of His Spirit: "Go ye into all the world and preach the gospel to every creature" (Mark 16:15, KJV)! We must obey now or forever be accountable for this generation. "How shall we escape if we neglect so great a salvation..." (Heb. 2:3).

If there has ever been a time to "fulfill your ministry," it's now. God is rattling the cages of our vision so that the gift and calling He's created in us may soar like they were created to soar. We're to bear fruit and reproduce. We must earnestly obey the holy calling and election He has given each of us—to reach the uttermost parts of the earth with His power and love, to shift the slipping tide of mankind to the feet of the Father, to convince the prodigal that there's more abundance in the Father's house, and to persuade the sinner of a Father's love, which knows no bounds or limits, so that they can be brought to the knowledge of salvation's grace. We must compel them to come in so our Father's house may be filled. We must fulfill our ministries; we must strive for the upward call in Christ Jesus. We must "cast our nets on the other side." Church, this is the day of salvation.

The gang member will renounce his vows to death when he's shown "life more abundantly." The prostitute will forsake her trade when she sees Jesus' face reflected in the bloodshot eyes of His own. The runaway will race to the arms of the Church when the heart of the Father is revealed. The junkie will throw away his needles when he's injected with the power of the Holy Spirit and the love of God through the needle of passion. The money-hungry businessman will sell all he has and give it to the poor when he's confronted with a destiny greater than his own. The woman on welfare who has had three abortions will consider her ways and repent when faced with the bloodstained love of Jesus through His Bride. This is the hour He's calling us to live what we believe—to demonstrate, not just imitate, His power and grace. The call is to all of us. The commission is to every Christian—the call is to you.

If any man will come after Me, let him deny himself, and take up his cross daily, and follow Me" (Luke 9:23, KJV).

"CRY OF THE SPIRIT IS HARVEST"

So the harvest of hearts sways to the sound of church bells,
Oblivious to the sound of eternity,
With no knowledge of Heaven or hell...

The child wanders the streets, with nothing to eat,
His heart hardened by life's severity,
Yearning, longing to lay it at the Master's feet.

The orphan and the widow search for a home,
Looking for God's eternal hope,
Begging from the streets not to be forgotten, alone...

The cry of the Spirit is "PREPARE!"
Cast out the nets and ropes!
The season to reap is here!

SPARE NOT! Lengthen your cords!
Cast your nets on the other side!
This is the day of the Lord!

Stretch out your curtains! Strengthen your stakes!
Get ready! Make haste!
As the levees of revival break!

This is the day the Lord has made!
To reap the harvest white,
To finish the race...

Launch out! Go into the fields!
Let your light so shine!
My power through you revealed!

Then the orphan and widow will say,
"Surely God is in you..."
By the love you show and the glory displayed...

The prisoner will exclaim
"You came unto me!
I was lost, but now I AM FREE!"

The blind man will shout,
"I can see! I can see!"
The skeptic will surely say, "I BELIEVE!"

The cry of the Spirit is, "PREPARE,
Cast out your nets and ropes,

The Harvest is here!
The Harvest is here!
The Harvest is here!"

CHAPTER 5

PREPARING

TO POSSESS

The early Church did not have promotion or propaganda. It did not have slogans and banners. It didn't have multimillion-dollar budgets and web pages. But one thing it did have was *power*. On that memorable day recorded in Acts chapter 3, we find Peter and John making their way to the temple to pray. They are met by a man begging for alms who has been lame from his mother's womb. If Peter and John were walking the streets today, the crippled man would have a sign that exclaimed: "Crippled. Need Food. God Bless," and he would confront them as they entered the grocery store or gas station. In this short exchange 2,000 years ago, we see a dynamic of the Kingdom of God that is rarely noticed in modern-day religion.

Power without glamour. Miracles without advertisement. Mass revival without mass promotion. These two early disciples had been with Christ. That was the secret of their success. They had watched the Master day after day and learned His attributes and habits. They had seen the miracles of Jesus and the innumerable crowds that followed Him. They had also seen the gimmicks of the Pharisees and their limited effect. They saw the religious manipulation in the temple that robbed from widows and the poor, to make the rich richer.

In Acts chapter 3 we find these two Christians at the gate of the temple. In the very same courts that still echo with the chants of, "Crucify Him! Crucify Him!" they now boldly demonstrate His majesty. In the streets where the threats and accusations of murder resounded is the power of life and love expressed through the simple people who followed Jesus. In this present hour of gross darkness and demonic threat, more than any other time in history, we need the demonstration of that divine love through those who follow Him. The world needs more than conferences and meetings, it needs miracles, signs, and wonders. It needs a people who have had a Mount of Transfiguration experience and enter the world shining.

There is only one way to really *know* Him. It's to be in that secret place *with* Him. God is looking for those who will abandon themselves to a life of prayer and devotion and who will honestly say with Peter, "Lo, we have left all, and have followed Thee" (Mark 10:28, KJV). God seeks people who esteem "the reproach of Christ greater riches than the treasures in Egypt" (Heb. 11:26, KJV) or the treasures of this passing, temporal world. Who will seek the place of prayer more than the place of leisure and pleasure? These are the ones who will change the course of history. These are the ones who will be written in the books of Heaven. It is you and I. It's anyone who will take up His cross and follow Him and who will *die* and let Him live inside. These are the ones who are known in hell. Their very steps cause the gates of Hades to tremble and quake. They are the children of the Most High God, who are crucified with Him, walking in resurrection power.

You see, first you must know the fellowship of His suffering before you can know the power of His resurrection. First you must eat of His flesh and drink of His blood before you can break that Bread for others. This invitation is to all of us, for all who will follow the Master. The call is for all who will give away the things of this frail life and pursue the one to come. It's an invitation to you and me: "And the Spirit and the bride say, 'Come!' And let him who hears say, 'Come!' And let him who thirsts, come. Whoever desires, let him take of the water of life freely" (Rev. 22:17).

We see a similar situation in the Book of Joshua. Joshua and all the tribes of Israel found themselves at the waters of the Jordan. They were thirsty not only for new springs to drink from and meat other than manna, but they were hungry and thirsty for the presence and power of God. They were a rugged generation who had seen the hardship and testing of the wilderness. They had only heard in legend and rhyme about the awesome power of the Lord of Hosts. Over and over they'd heard about the wonders of God demonstrated to their forefathers. They were hungry for their own experience, to see Him for themselves. Like Moses, they were crying out, "*Show* ME Your glory!"

As they gathered at the Jordan, they were in a state of preparation, anticipation, and expectation to finally see the promises they'd heard of for so long. They were promised in Joshua 1:11 (KJV) that they would finally see the Promised Land: "Pass through the host, and command the people, saying, *prepare* you victuals; for within three days ye shall pass over this Jordan, to go in to possess the land, which the Lord your God giveth you to possess it." They left Egypt laden down with gold and riches only to wander for 40 years, poor and wretched. Now all that they clutched in their hands and hearts were the promises of God and a hunger to see them fulfilled. We are in this same process today. We have been sunk by the weight of prosperity teaching, which has left our compassion shipwrecked.

Now a breed of men and women have taken center stage who have a new message, "Silver and gold [we] do not have, *but what [we] do have [we] give you...rise up and walk*" (Acts 3:6). They are a people filled with love, not only knowledge; power, not only words; and action, not only religion. They have one thing on their minds—the nations of the world, the uttermost parts of the earth. They are crossing the Jordan of circumstance and are invading the kingdoms of this world. They carry the torch of history's revivals and awakenings and know that God said:

Ask of Me, and I shall give Thee the heathen for Thine inheritance, and the uttermost parts of the earth for Thy possession (Psalm 2:8, KJV).

The preparation is for the demonstration so that we can be a people not only of word, but also of power. We have practiced behind closed doors for long enough! It's time to display and demonstrate the truth we've believed for so long. It's time to take the new wine out into the streets and spill it until the streets are drunk with it. What is the wine and oil for? Is it not to pour out into the wounds of the one beaten and left for dead on the side of the road? Who will be the world's neighbor in this hour? Who will ignore his own flesh and its demand for comfort to dare the cold, wind, and rain and leave the 99 for the 1? Listen to Jeremiah and let it pierce your heart! "Arise, cry out in the night...pour out your heart like water before the face of the Lord. Lift up your hands toward Him for the lives of your young children, who faint from hunger at the head of every street" (Lam. 2:19).

The word translated as *street* in that verse comes from a Hebrew word *chuwts* (khoots), which means literally, "separated by a wall, i.e. outside, outdoors." An alternate meaning is "abroad, a field, or highway." To go to the streets is to go beyond the confines of our habitations and beyond the boundaries of our church buildings to demonstrate to a lost world the love of an eternal Father who gave ALL for even ONE of them. "In this was manifested the love of God toward us, because God sent His only begotten Son into the world, that we might live through Him" (1 John 4:9, KJV).

So, as the army of the Lord, we find ourselves at a prophetic junction. He has assembled us at the waters of decision to cross over and possess the land He has given us, or to stay in the wilderness of tradition and die. The entire creation awaits our response. The nations weigh in the balances of our obedience. Will we be like the rich young ruler who gave in to the arguments of this world, or like the soldiers whom the apostle Paul spoke of, "You therefore must endure hardship as a good soldier of Jesus Christ. No one engaged in warfare entangles himself with the affairs of this life, that he may please him who enlisted him as a soldier" (2 Tim. 2:3-4).

If we engage in the spiritual struggle of the age, we must disengage from this fleeting futile world and "seek first the kingdom of God" (Matt. 6:33, KJV), "looking unto Jesus, the author and finisher of our faith" (Heb. 12:2, KJV). We must, "deny ourselves, take up the cross, and follow Him" (see Luke 9:23). This is the résumé of the army that will cause the gates of hell to tremble and break, cause the very earth to shudder and shake, and cause the sinner and skeptic to contemplate the power and majesty of the Most High God manifested in and through His saints!

But now in Joshua 18:3 we see a paradox. Here was a land that had been given to Israel by God Himself. They had already seen the victory in the plains of Jericho, and numerous other battles were won hands-down. Yet in just a few short years we find Israel in a compromising state. "And Joshua said to the children of Israel, '*How long will you neglect to go and possess the land* which the Lord God of your fathers has given you?' " (Josh. 18:3) How long? How long will we neglect the God-given command to each of us, to "*go therefore and make disciples of all nations*" (Matt. 28:19)?

How long? Have we so soon forgotten the promise of God to those He has called? *"Ask of Me, and I will give You the nations for Your inheritance, and the ends of the earth for Your possession"* (Ps. 2:8). How long, my friend, will we wait to do the job God has called each of us to do? To "occupy till I come" (Luke 19:13, KJV). I say again, "HOW LONG?"

My eyes still wander to and fro,
For those who surely know that I am coming soon.
To strongly uphold these hearts that are Mine,
That await My coming in the sky,
Hastening the coming day of the Lord,
Occupying the land and engaging in war....

CHAPTER 6

THE CROSS WE
MUST CARRY IS HIS

The Cross was the personal signature of God's grace. It was a public declaration of His love for the sinner, the outcast, and the hungry. It was a demonstration of unprecedented clarity of His power over death and sin to save to the uttermost. He lifted up the banner of His mercy and, in doing so, draws all men unto Himself. He is a selfless, sacrificial, spotless, sinless offering of truth.

The Cross is the enduring landmark across the landscape of time, testifying of God's unconditional compassion for the human race. His long arm reaches into the darkest deep and snatches the soul from the mire of self and sin. Of this very Cross, He says to us, "Take it up and follow Me." Only the scars of this Cross in one's soul give access into hell to retrieve treasures out of darkness, "translating them into the Kingdom of His dear Son" (see Col. 1:13).

Without the testimony of the Cross, there's no recognition in hell or Heaven. This Paul preached, "For it pleased the Father that in Him all the fullness should dwell, and by Him to reconcile all things to Himself, by Him, whether things on earth or things in heaven, having made peace through the blood of His cross" (Col. 1:19-20). To say "I'm a Christian" isn't enough. To take up your cross, deny yourself, and follow His life of evangelism and ministry is. When He declared that the things He did we will do as well, He wasn't just boasting of our good deeds and great accomplishments. What He literally said was, "The things I have done, the kind of life I've lived, the blood I have given, the time I've expended, you will do too."

The Cross is a life of evangelism. The Cross is a life of giving more than you receive, pouring out more than you take in. It's a life of passion. It's caring for the sick and the orphaned; it's opening your house to a stranger. It's sheltering the widow and visiting them in their affliction. The life of Jesus kissed the Cross. The life of the Christian must make the same embrace of sacrifice and death. To go through the Cross with your dreams and ambitions is to taste and experience His resurrection power, not only in your own life but also in the lives of everyone you touch. "For the message of the cross is foolishness to those who are perishing, but to us who are being saved it is the power of God" (1 Cor. 1:18).

The Cross is the consummation of all that God is. "For God loved the world so much He gave..." (John 3:16). The Cross is the smile of God upon a lost and dying world. The Cross is the stamp of God's approval on a world that failed. The Cross is the heart of God revealed in its blood, guts, and glory. The Cross is Jesus. With it we will remind a hell-bent world and a jealous grave of the Father's eternal intention for mankind—mercy. With it we will loose every prisoner from his chains of despair. With it we will declare to the world that God still reaches for all people with pierced and bleeding hands. With it we will brand every lonely heart with His death-defying love and set it free.

It's a power so strong that it will melt the heart of a maddened criminal scarred by life's cruelties. Like the thief he will cry out at the sight of the bloody Cross, "Remember me!" It is a power so overwhelming that it will bring ruthless thugs to their knees in repentance, crying out at His appearance, "Surely this was the Son of God" (see Matt. 27:54). The abusive, rejected father will melt at the fire of His passion for him and will bow at this Cross with the words, "Father forgive them, for they know not what they do" (Luke 23:34, KJV). It's the brutal, bloody cross of Calvary that will positively set the captive free! Again He asks, *"Have you taken up your cross?"*

It's a life less pampered, but more powerful. It's nights of less sleep, but filling many hearts with salvation. There will be years of toil, but oh the triumph! There is less luxury, but an abundant life! We will bear painful scars, but the joy of the Holy Ghost! The Cross is the trophy of grace that the heart must wear to truly say, "I have kept the faith, I have finished my course" (2 Tim. 4:7, KJV). Let's be champions of the Cross, boldly declaring His act of love to the masses until we hear at the finish: "Come, you blessed of My Father, inherit the kingdom prepared for you from the foundation of the world: for I was hungry and you gave Me food; I was thirsty and you gave Me drink; I was a stranger and you took Me in; I was naked and you clothed Me; I was sick and you visited Me; I was in prison and you came unto Me" (Matt. 25:34-36).

"For many walk, of whom I have told you often, and now tell you even weeping, that they are the enemies of the cross of Christ" (Phil. 3:18). They were not enemies of Christ so to speak. They were enemies of His cross and of His life and selfless sacrifice. They were foes of the furtherance of the gospel, lovers of self more than lovers of God. O Lord! Give us an army in love with Your cross! Give us Christians who are passionate for the lost and who will follow You at any cost! We must carry His cross!

I was walking down the avenue;
It must have been around midnight.
I saw the homeless and the destitute;
They looked at me through dying eyes.

One man asked me for a dollar,
Said he hadn't eaten in three days;
Spends his nights at the Greyhound,
His ticket to misery says "One Way."

In that old man's eyes,
To my great surprise,
Suddenly I saw Jesus!

In his old grizzled hands,
It was hard to understand,
How I could see the nail prints!

In that old man's eyes,
Past life's cheap disguise,
I could see Jesus.

In that old man's hands,
I can finally understand,
How I could see the nail prints.

CHAPTER 7

THE FRUIT
OF REVIVAL

In any move of God, the level of impact is generally measured by the fruit that remains after the initial experience. Jesus made it clear at the consummation of His earthly ministry that He hadn't lost even one who was entrusted to Him (see John 17:12). The measure of His ministry was the fruit that remained. Jesus taught: "I chose you and appointed you that you should go and bear fruit, and that your fruit should remain" (John 15:16). Revival is something that so powerfully affects a city, a street, a home, a nation, or a person that they are forever changed under the weight of glory revealed.

Revival isn't a three-day event that we advertise as "Revival." It's not a state of mind, but rather a state of perpetual impact that drastically changes the moral climate of an area. The way people think in that region changes. The way people treat each other changes. The fog of deception begins to lift and the "eyes of your understanding are enlightened" (see Eph. 1:18). Revival is an experience, not a definition. It can't be germinated in a test tube of theology; it can only be demonstrated by radical obedience through those who pursue it. It deals with people, not statistics.

Revival forces the issue of commitment. It deals with the heart of the Church and measures the level of compassion. It's the measuring stick of passion. Go to a city's street and you'll find the pulse of the city's church. See the intensity of the light and witness of Christ in the marketplace and you'll determine the intensity of devotion and obedience in the church place. If you find the church on the streets Monday through Saturday, then you'll surely find Christ in their midst on Sunday. You can't have one without the other—street and revival are inseparable.

Revival doesn't look like we expect it to look. Revival is shocking. It never dresses the same and never smells the same— it's unorthodox. It's unreligious. It surprises; it's hardly ever invited or expected. It comes on its own terms and in its own way, suddenly. And it doesn't always wear the face we expect. It can be painted black or white; it may have piercings and tattoos. It may smell like urine or fancy cologne. It shows up on Sunday morning in the middle of a well thought-out sermon. It comes and sits at our feet and begs for a piece of bread. It comes to us in its worst while we're at our best. It demands more than we have to give. It demands God.

Revival is waiting for us on the streets. It's hiding from us in nursing homes and prisons. It's calling to us from foreign fields and obscure places. It is crying, yearning for even one person who will rise from the confines of normality and pursue it. It's looking for a person who will approach the throne of grace with boldness and expect a miracle and who will stand on a street corner and wait for its shadow to pass by, knowing that at any minute the wind that blows where it wants to may touch down in that very spot, exploding and expanding everything it touches. Revival is a fire, and souls are its kindling.

Places like Brownsville (and the revival evident there) are only glimpses of what we're about to experience globally—it was a forerunner to the greater works. It was the firstfruits of a chosen generation, a peculiar people. All over the land we're about to see these fires burning in the nameless and faceless average people who don't have fame or notoriety. Bars will become revival centers. Barns will become training centers. Brothels and barrios will be flaming agents of His grace. Insane asylums and mental wards will be the instruments of power and glory. The world as we know it is about to be changed. Revival is about to visit the land.

We are the catalysts of this fire. We are the riverbeds that this torrent comes through. We are the gatekeepers who must cry out, "Here am I, send me!" Revival is not a hand on a clock waiting for the alarm to sound. It's the ever-beating heart of every person who contains the treasure of eternal life—that hope of glory, Christ in us. Once we begin to step from the porches of tradition into the ghetto of the impossible, we'll begin to see His unprecedented power. It's through our hands that He desires to demonstrate His glory. It's through our lips that He longs to express His personality. We are revival.

Historical revivals are only seeds of a great harvest about to spring up. They are only landmarks compelling us "toward the goal for the prize of the upward call of God in Christ Jesus" (see Phil. 3:14). We must at all cost, "forget the things that are behind us, and reach forward to those things that lie ahead" (see Phil. 3:13). It's only there that we will experience His glory. It's only there that we'll see the impossible become tangible, the unreal a reality, and the uncomely become royalty. God is calling to an army of revivalists who will step out into their cities and begin to believe. We must believe that "[He] is able to do exceeding abundantly above all that we ask or think..." (Eph. 3:20, KJV). God is looking for people who believe the unbelievable and in return receive "treasures out of darkness" reserved for such a time as this. This is the fruit of revival. He is the vine and we are the branches.

CHAPTER 8

REFORMATION BEFORE REVIVAL!

On October 31, 1517, Martin Luther, the German monk who was born a peasant in Eisleben, Germany, began what some would call a revolution. It was a revolution in religious thought and spiritual canon—a grass-roots revival that brought the freedom of salvation to thousands, even millions. But what Luther opposed is much more critical than the man himself. If he's forgotten, we lose nothing. But if what he opposed is forgotten, we're in danger of falling into the same pit and snare that the Church was in 500 years ago. God forbid, if we haven't already.

On October 31, 1517, Luther nailed the 95 Theses to the Castle Church door in Wittenberg, thus bringing him the infamous title of heretic and ruffian—enemy of the church of Rome and Germany. How this came about is even more shocking. Luther confronted the use of indulgences, defined as "a release from the temporal penalties for sin through the payment of money." These indulgences were being sold to raise money to build Saint Peter's Basilica in Rome, paid for by the sweat of the common man on the basis of false hope and fear for loved ones trapped in purgatory. Martin Luther cried out to the common peasant and citizen of Germany:

> "Christians are to be taught that it would be the pope's wish, as it is his duty, to give of his own money to very many of those from whom certain hawkers of pardons cajole money, even though the church of St. Peter might have to be sold" (Martin Luther's Thesis 51).

Today, the Church finds itself at the same crossroads. We're told if we pay enough, spend enough, give enough, and tithe enough, we'll somehow be rewarded in this life and in the one to come with great and lofty things. By doing this, we'll secure greater access to Heaven than we had before. In giving money, we will find riches for family and ourselves and all the while these churches and ministries grow larger than life itself while the streets and alleys of our cities and towns are left utterly forsaken. The orphan and the widow go unattended and unvisited. Still the gangs and children "faint for hunger at the top of every street" (see Lam. 2:19) while "nobles" grow richer on the hard work and sweat of the common man. Conferences charge hundreds of dollars per person to meet unnecessary budgets, and still the streets hear only an echo of what's preached there. Inspiration has become an institution, and the institution has become an industry.

Resembling a circus at times, the conference comes to town with flashing lights, declaring its procession of names and celebrities, drawing the crowd and charging the money, forgetting that Jesus Himself set an example for us to follow: "When you give a dinner or a supper, do not ask your friends, your brothers, your relatives, nor your rich neighbors.... But when you give a feast, invite the poor, the maimed, the lame, the blind. And you will be blessed..." (Luke 14:12-14).

The reason we don't have revival in our cities and our nation is that we haven't had a reformation first! We haven't had the revelation of who Jesus really is, which will lead to revolution. Somewhere in his pursuit of knowledge and peace of mind, Martin Luther came to a revelation of Jesus Christ. From that shred of truth came a revolution. It led to a spiritual revival from dead works and greedy practices. It gave back salvation and liberty in the Holy Ghost to the common man. It fed the people the unleavened bread of simplicity instead of the rotten manna of men's thinking and reasoning. Only in a revelation of that simplicity will we find the revolution that will change our crime-ridden, gang-infested streets to rivers of living water. Only at the feet of Jesus Himself will we be empowered to make the impact harvest demands. The cry is:

> "Christians are to be taught that he who gives to the poor or lends to the needy does a better work than buying pardons. Christians are to be taught that he who sees a man in need, and passes him by, and gives his money for pardons, purchases not the indulgences of the pope, but the indignation of God" (Martin Luther's Theses 43 and 45).

We must move beyond conference to confrontation. We must take off the garments of enterprise and put on the garments of eternity, seeking first the Kingdom of God. The word *revolution* means "a radical change in thought." We must make a radical change in our thinking and approach the throne of grace with boldness. No longer should we bring petitions of grandeur and gain, but rather, we must cry out, "*Give me souls or give me death!*" Then and only then will we see the revival that we long for. For if we really longed for it then we wouldn't hesitate to pay the price to secure it.

> "Away, then, with all those prophets who say to the people of Christ, 'Peace, peace,' and there is no peace! Blessed be all those prophets who say to the people of

Christ, 'Cross, cross,' and there is no cross!" (Martin Luther's Theses 92 and 93).

Weeping even as he spoke, Paul said in Philippians that there were some who were the "enemies of the cross of Christ" (Phil. 3:18, KJV). They weren't enemies necessarily of Jesus Himself; they probably followed Him from town to town just to get something from Him. But they were enemies of the *CROSS OF CHRIST! They were enemies of the lifestyle of Jesus, the sacrifice, the denial of oneself. And thus, this made them enemies of Him!* Today, many embrace the doctrines of Jesus; they applaud Him every Sunday; they wear T-shirts and necklaces that advertise Him, but they refuse to take up their cross and *follow Him*!

> "They are enemies of Christ and of the pope, who bid the Word of God be altogether silent in some churches, in order that pardons may be preached in others" (Martin Luther's Thesis 53).

Revival will come when a reformation of religion comes first. We've seen the firstfruits in some places, but God knows a spiritual revolution still awaits us, a revolution that will shake institutions and intuitions. A revolution that will change the way we approach the throne of grace and that will reform and renew our minds, transforming the way we judge those who may be of a different denomination or doctrinal statement. Reformation will clean out the closets of the Church and what will emerge is a purified Bride ready for the Bridegroom. "Let the bridegroom go out from his chamber, and the bride from her dressing room. Let the priests, who minister to the Lord, weep between the porch and the altar; let them say, 'Spare Your people, O Lord! And do not give Your heritage to reproach' " (Joel 2:16-17a).

CHAPTER 9

VIOLENCE
FOR THE VISION

Jesus Christ was the epitome of violence for the vision. Though a Roman cross cast its dark shadow across His future, He saw what lay ahead and His perfect love for you and me cast out all images of fear and terror. He embraced suffering to see the fulfillment of His Father's will. Yet, in this hour it seems very few will taste this fellowship to see their vision come to fruition. They are satisfied to live in the shadow of another and never pursue their own. We need violence for the vision! Like Jacob, we need to wrestle with destiny and receive the blessing to invade the land and conquer! Like Paul, we need our days in the deep to hear His voice speaking our name and appearing to us for our purpose (see Acts 26:16-18).

"Where there is no revelation, the people cast off restraint" (Prov. 29:18a). King Solomon states again, "Where there is no vision, the people perish" (Prov. 29:18, KJV). We are in a state of "no restraint" in the land! Why? Because of the lack of divine vision and personal prophetic revelation. We lack an intimacy with the Father that produces divine power. We no longer go to Him, but rather we catch the latest popular wave and ride it into the shores of mediocrity. We're never willing to pay the price for personal revelation and vision. We're content to walk in the foot-steps of another instead of following His steps up the mountain of transfiguration and vision. *We need violence for our own vision!*

In First Samuel we witness an interesting event. The voice of the Lord calls out for Samuel, and he immediately arises and goes to Eli, responding, "Here I am!" Samuel doesn't even com-prehend that it is the Lord longing for his attention! How long have you heard His voice calling your name, yet you've run to the face of man, not to the feet of God? He's still calling to you and me, longing to anoint us and send us even as He did Samuel so long ago. He's still looking for kings and priests to wait on Him in the inner courts of His presence. We must respond as Samuel finally did: "Now the Lord came and stood and called as at other times, 'Samuel! Samuel!' And Samuel answered, 'Speak, for Your servant hears' " (1 Sam. 3:10).

This hour demands revelation and vision from the Father's heart. Like no other time in history, there is such a demand for a clear understanding of the times. Yet we find ourselves in a moral breakdown and crisis. Might it be said then, that where there's no prayer the people perish? "But the end of all things is at hand: be ye therefore sober, and *watch* unto prayer" (1 Pet. 4:7, KJV). Prayer and communion with the Spirit, personally and corporately, are our spiritual eyes to see. Without them we're the blind leading the blind. The revival that must first touch the land is the revival of prayer and devotion between the Church and her Father. In that revival we'll find the power to transform our streets and cities. In that revival we'll find the violence for the vision. We'll find ourselves wrestling not with flesh and blood, but with anything that would try to keep us from that most holy place at His side and on His chest, hearing His urgent heartbeat for the nations of the world.

Jesus longs for us to spend time in prayer:

And being in agony, He prayed more earnestly. Then His sweat became like great drops of blood falling down to the ground. When He arose from prayer, and came to His disciples, He found them sleeping from sorrow. Then He said to them, "Why do you sleep? Rise and pray, lest you enter into temptation" (Luke 22:44-46).

The ones who will face the giants and slay them are the ones who have first faced their God and loved Him. The ones who will move nations and principalities have first moved the heart of God with their intercessions and prayers. Only the wilderness of testing will produce a message of power and authority that will leave the masses speechless. Only when we spend time with Him will the masses say, "They have been with Christ." Can we do any less now? The Spirit makes intercession for us knowing our weaknesses. I wonder what He says? I doubt if it's any different from what Jesus said: "Rise and pray! Spend time with Me and then go change your streets and cities! Everywhere you go, preach, saying, the Kingdom of God is at hand [it's attainable, within reach, tangible], pray for the sick, raise the dead, cast out demons, freely you have received, now freely give" (see Matt. 10:7-8).

In this hour, prayer will prepare the warriors of the Cross to be marked by holy violence. They will not quit no matter the cost to time, money, or any other personal thing. They'll endure to the end, and thus be saved. They will climb any mountain, cross any sea, and dare any enemy to defy the one Most High God. They are the ones who will cry out with David, "Is there not a cause" (1 Sam. 17:29, KJV). The cause of Christ will beat in their veins just as the instinct to fly pulses in the heart of an eagle. They'll mount up to do the works of Jesus their Master.

They will possess the land. They'll occupy till He comes. They'll love not their own lives, even to death. They'll count all things as dung to gain Him. They'll be a people who will hazard their lives for the sake of the gospel, leaving their nets and their living to follow Him and to *go* and preach the Kingdom of God! This is you! This is me! *We* are that chosen generation! *We* are that royal priesthood! *We* are that peculiar people zealous of good works! *We* are the ones He has created for good works in Christ Jesus! We are the ones to consummate the end of the age! Let's go do this and so much more! Let's run the race with reckless abandon, knowing that "to live is Christ and to die is gain" (Phil. 1:21, KJV).

> *Is there any who wrestle in the night?*
> *Who love Me more than this present life?*
> *Who will wait on Me in the secret place,*
> *To touch Me, to see My face?*
> *Who will fly to unknown places?*
> *Who will go with power to the nations?*
> *To take the precious seed,*
> *That the children may believe?*
> *Will any eagles dare the storm?*
> *That destiny and vision can be born?*
> *To fly above the winds of tradition,*
> *To have purpose, to have vision?*
> *Who will give ear for the time to come?*
> *That those who read it may run?*
> *To see the dream and understand,*
> *To be the salt that preserves the land?*
> *Come, My beloved, to the secret place!*
> *There we will dance; there we will embrace!*
> *I will show you things to come,*
> *In that place our hearts will become one!*
> *And you will be My voice to the nations!*
> *I will take you to the highest places!*

Of My Spirit you will taste,
To behold My unveiled face!
You are Mine!
Arise now and shine!
Let the world see your light!
Let the children know that there is hope in Christ.

I pray only that these words take on a life of their own and activate the divine destiny within you. I pray that the shepherd boy will see that he's a king, that the little girl will comprehend she's a bride, espoused to a King—the King of kings and Lord of lords! I pray that you will realize that you are the apple of His eye; for you He died and for you He gave His life.

Now, take your vision with violence. "And from the days of John the Baptist until now the kingdom of heaven suffers violence, and the violent take it by force" (Matt. 11:12).

CHAPTER 10

ADDICTED
TO THE GLORY

I'll never forget the first time I stepped out of my grand-father's house after being saved to take the love that had just exploded in my heart to the streets. From house to house I went, knocking on every door with the same line, "Do you want to talk about Jesus?" Then I finally went back to the same neighbor-hood where, just days before, I had been dealing drugs and ped-dling stolen jewelry for cocaine. Dozens of kids, drug dealers, and junkies gathered around to hear this strange sound: "Jesus loves you, man."

I'll never forget watching these people bow down on the concrete in broad daylight to ask Jesus into their hearts even as I did hours before. They sobbed and cried out to the Lord right there on the streets. Grown men and women were smitten by a Power that transcended all despair and sin, piercing their heart and soul. The manifest presence of the Lord causes skeptics to be transformed into saints, prostitutes into princesses, and rebels into righteous radicals. I was becoming addicted to the glory of God.

I witnessed His glory in the first few days of my salvation experience with Jesus. I became hooked on the passion and power of the Lord as waitresses bowed at the end of the table and accepted Him as Lord and Master and as hardened criminals sat at the foot of the cell bed and wept like babies as they repented for their sins. Like a junkie sticks a needle into his vein for that jolt, that rush, I became a junkie for the demonstration of Jesus' love and power as they came into contact with a sinner. I was hooked. I was addicted.

Jesus wasn't just a systematic theology. He was a living and breathing Person, eager to share His love with the world! He wasn't lethargic and full of ritual and repetition. He was excited and spontaneous in His expression of the Father's love. I found myself quickly following His lead. I remember one time that, in the excitement of it all, I jumped from my Christian friend's car, ran toward a guy walking down the street, and yelled, "Jesus loves you, man! Jesus really loves you!" Later that night, the same guy told the church that he had been on his way to kill a man who was messing with his girlfriend! That impulsive encounter literally saved a life! I was addicted. I became forever hooked on the power of God that is demonstrated when darkness and light collide—when a broken, hardened heart accepts Jesus' love.

Once, after spending most of the night preaching from street corner to street corner in downtown Seattle in 1988, we started making our way back home. When we hit First Avenue and Pioneer Square, we stopped the car and got out for a moment to pray and ask God's blessing on our evening. It was around four in the morning. My friend, David, began softly singing "Amazing Grace." As we reached the chorus, suddenly a dozen or more street people crawled from the bushes and came from the shadows to lock hands with us and sing the song: "How sweet the sound, that saved a wretch like me. I once was lost but now am found, was blind, but now I see." We were stunned as this misfit choir awoke to His glory and came to lift their voices and praise Him at four in the morning with only the angels and Heaven to witness this divine assembly. We were addicted to the awesome glory of the Lord.

I believe that's what Paul meant when he said, "Woe is me if I preach not the gospel" (see 1 Cor. 9:16). Those are the words of an addict, someone overcome with a Thing, a Person, and a Power that flows through mere human hands to open blind eyes and raise dead bodies. Paul was addicted to the glory of God, which is why he said, "This one thing I do, I forget the things that are behind me and reach forward to what lies ahead of me. I strive for the upward call in Christ Jesus" (see Phil. 3:13).

An addict can never have enough. He always needs more. As his tolerance level rises, he is forced to feed his habit with an increased amount of that substance. It's no wonder that Paul exhorted, "But we all, with unveiled face, beholding as in a mirror the glory of the Lord, are being transformed into the same image from glory to glory" (2 Cor. 3:18). One taste wasn't enough; one encounter with a crippled person wasn't enough; one confrontation in the synagogue didn't satisfy his craving. He had to have more! Paul was an addict; he was forever hooked on the glory and power of his Master, Jesus Christ. God give us an army of addicts!

If your relationship and devotion to the Lord have become predictable and boring, I dare you to find a stranger anywhere and share the love that the Lord has so abundantly shed abroad in your heart! Give away what's been freely given to you and you, too, will find yourself hooked on the glory, which, in seconds, can turn a derelict into a disciple, a pimp into a preacher, and a beggar into a prophet. Break out of the conformed walls of your religion and begin to shout from the housetops what Jesus has whispered in your hearts! Let the whole world know what He has done for you! And in that very moment, you'll become an addict of His glory as so many already are!

You, too, will shout with a voice of triumph, and the sound of singing will be heard in the streets of your city or town! A river of revival will flow from your heart and wash away the needles and beer cans that litter your streets and neighborhoods. Only then will we see the harvest that our hearts have longed for. Only when we all become addicted to Jesus' power will we see the power and glory of God shake the land as in days of old. God, give us an army of addicts who are addicted to Your glory and who can't sleep or rest until they've seen Your power and passion shake this nation. Let the fire of Your desire burn in their veins until they've fully satisfied that craving for more of You. Meet them, Lord; meet them on the highways and byways, and show them Your glory."

"The Least of These…"

Now a young man sits in a jail cell,
no longer is his heart compelled.
So he lays his head down tonight,
wondering if he'll even see the morning light…
A little girl sits on a corner street,
shivering from the cold and begging for something to eat.
She doesn't know where her daddy's gone;
she just lays her head down and waits for the dawn…
A little baby is sleeping in a crib alone,
crying for some milk because mama's not home.
There's a needle on the counter where the bottle should be,
but no one's around to hear this baby's plea…
There's an old man sleeping on a bench tonight,
for the bottle he's lost his kids and wife.
He prays only that someone will try to understand,
reach out and give him a helping hand…
Jesus said to help the least of these,

the ones who are lost and dying in the streets.
The prisoner and the runaway,
we've got to reach out and show them the Way...
Cast your nets on the other side;
the fields of harvest are white.
And then the revelation of why Jesus died,
a fisher of men, a thief in the night...
When I was cold you put shoes on my feet;
when I was hungry you gave something to eat.
When I was desperate, forgotten, and alone,
you opened up your hearts and you opened up your home.
When you do it to the least of these,
You have really done it unto Me.

(See Matthew 25:31-46.)

CHAPTER 11

THE VALUE OF A SOUL

"Again, the devil took Him up into an exceedingly high mountain, and showed Him all the kingdoms of the world and the glory of them; and said to Him, 'All these things will I give You if You will fall down and worship me' " (Matt. 4: 8-9). Satan so intensely comprehended the value of one soul that he was willing to wager all he had on one. He would pay any price to secure this eternal transaction. A billion dollars was and is not enough to spend in satan's greed for souls. Yet today, the Church is hardly moved to see souls saved, unwilling to expend a small margin of their budget to capture the heart of even one person who is lost and dying. We have lost the priceless value of a soul.

When Jesus confronted the rich young ruler He said, "Sell all that you have and distribute to the poor" (see Luke 18:22). But the young man was already bought. Satan had already paid his own ransom—the riches and wealth of this present world. Likewise, every second another soul is purchased and paid for with the "kingdoms of this world and the glory of them" (see

Matt. 4:8). In comparison, so little is expended by God's people for the purchase of even one precious soul. Satan has the riches and wealth of the world at his disposal, but we have the blood of Jesus. The reason we do not give our lives and wealth for the Son of God and His epic passion for souls is because we have not grasped the great value of one. Satan does, and alas, the mouth of hell expands to accommodate the influx.

For example, Luke 16:19-23 tells the story of a rich man whom satan courted with wealth and fame, seducing his soul into hell. "There was a certain rich man, who was clothed in purple and fine clothes, and lived in splendor every day. The rich man also died and was buried, and in hell he lifted up his eyes." There is no price tag too large that satan is unwilling to pay in order to secure one soul into damnation. Tragically, today we will hardly give our time and energy, not to mention our money, to see someone saved. The current price tags on our favorite conferences and meetings already bankrupt us. We have nothing left with which to feed the hungry, clothe the naked, or bring the stranger into our home. Every day we walk past the priceless treasure of souls, unwilling to pay the price to see them saved. We are at a terrible disadvantage because satan is not as nonchalant as we are.

God, however, is even more passionate to win souls than satan is. John 3:16 tells us that God was willing to pay the ultimate price to save souls: "For God so loved the world that He gave His only begotten Son." Heaven understands the value of a soul. The Father paid the highest possible price—His only Son—to apprehend one soul for eternity. What will we do? What price is too much for us to give for missions and harvest? Where is the limit in our giving to see our cities and streets won to Christ? Where do we stop to see the widow and the orphan delivered from their affliction? It cost Jesus everything. It will cost us no less. The burning question in God's heart is, "What will you give for a soul? What have you given lately for a soul?"

We must not be caught up in the trappings of wealth. Luke 12:16-21 tells the story of a person who was. "The ground of a certain rich man yielded plentifully...so he said, 'I will do this: I will pull down my barns and build greater...And I will say to my soul, "Soul, you have many goods laid up for many years; take your ease; eat, drink, and be merry." ' But God said to him, 'Fool! This night your soul will be required of you.' " The only value in wealth is to use it for the furtherance of the Kingdom of God and to enable it to be the catalyst that empowers outreach and revival. In so doing, we obey Christ's command in Matthew 6:19-21 (KJV), which says, "Lay not up for yourselves treasures upon earth...but lay up for yourselves treasures in heaven...for where your treasure is, there will your heart be also." This was Jesus' strategy for prosperity. Our treasure in Heaven will be the souls that were saved and the hearts that were bound up with His eternal love during our lifetime.

Again we read about the folly of trading a soul for earthly riches: "For what does a man profit if he gains the whole world but loses his own soul? Or what shall a man give in exchange for his soul" (Matt. 1:26). Heaven and hell understand this principle and the value of a soul. It was this principle that compelled Jesus to the cross. It is the same force that will move us to take up our own cross and follow Him into the harvest fields. We must comprehend the value of a soul if we are ever going to enjoy the benefits and blessings of revival! Only then will we move with fervent desire to see souls saved. Only then will we break out of the confinement of human limitations into the divine presence of revival. God, give us a passion for souls!

CHAPTER 12

A Cry for Destiny

This is a generation of people that longs for demonstration, not imagination. They want the real thing. In order to reach them, we must meet them where *they* are, not where *we* are. We must take down the advertisements we so proudly fly that give the idea, "You come to us on our terms or don't bother coming at all. You must see Jesus as we see Him or you just can't have Him. You will dress like us, act like us, and most certainly believe like us."

It's no wonder we're losing an entire generation to animated heroes on TV and con men on the street corners. We've built a steeple that's too high to attain! We've taken the manger and built a cathedral. All the while, people perish. As we continue to build higher and higher, an entire generation sinks in the mire of religion and apathy, never knowing who they are and why they were born. Before millions more perish in hopelessness, we must "condescend to these of low estate" (see Rom. 12:16) and give them the reality of Jesus Christ in all its blood and guts, scourging and mocking, death and resurrection. We must take off the mask of doctrinal indifference and reveal to them the scars.

Now's the time to shout down the fortified walls of clerical callousness and cry out "GRACE, GRACE!" in the face of the mountain of sin that threatens to landslide our youths into oblivion. We must go to them NOW and show them a Christ who's living and breathing and filled with compassion for their future. We must throw off the starched collar of religion and bleed as He bled for their lives and souls.

First, we must meet them on their own turf—with their own sound and their own feel. We must show them we care enough to accept them as they are, as Christ did. Then we must give them the anointing, not mere religion. The anointing, delivered in love, will break every yoke. Religion is a frequency they don't understand; they perceive only the unadulterated power of God. This is their language, their creed. They desire His power and His love. They need destiny—that's what will change them. We must show them who they are, who they could be, and where they are going in Christ.

They need to hear a sound they haven't heard, but that they long to hear. Even as the multitudes were astounded 2,000 years ago when they heard Jesus preaching in the streets, because He spoke as no other man spoke, so the multitudes today must hear a sound no man could fabricate or duplicate—the sound of a mighty rushing wind, the sound of Heaven. This is the sound that will arrest their hearts and convince them of their dire need for His love and grace. The only question is, will there be any who will have the courage to step outside the confines of "church" as we understand it and show them the real thing? Will anyone take to them the purity and passion of the King?

They long for a sound, a sign, and a landmark to show them the Way in this gross darkness. This generation is waiting for the sound of their call and destiny, and hell better beware when they do! They'll usher in the coming of Christ—first, in their passion and desire for Him, and then, in the sky.

Who will give heed to this? Who will give ear to the time to come? Who will sweat and bleed for the least of these? Who will give ear to the cry of the orphan and widow? Will we stand by, idle and dumb, as they die? Will the ox fall into the pit of despair as we rest? Or will we rise up in vehement desire to see them saved and redeemed? Must we hear the words of the Master, "I never knew you…" (Matt. 7:23)?

Now is the time for passion—passion for the heart of the Father, passion for His desire—to hear the cry of His heart and respond, "*Here am I, send me!*" A milling, scuffling, shifting tide of humanity awaits our quickening. The lost await the man, the woman, the child who will say, "I am crucified with Christ. It is no longer I who live but He that lives in me" (see Gal. 2:20). How long will we wait to fulfill the ministry with which He's entrusted us? Paul said he was "*trusted* with the gospel he preached" (see 1 Cor. 9:16-17), and woe to him if he didn't preach it!

When will we shake off the dust of church policy and invade a desperate, dying world with His blazing love and compassion? Who will seek the favor of God more than the fading, fake favor of man? Paul was bold to proclaim, "For do I now persuade men, or God? Or do I seek to please men? *For if I still pleased men, I would not be a bondservant of Christ*" (Gal. 1:10). This generation needs that kind of love! They need Christians who will dare to share and who will go to them and show them the reality of Jesus in earthen vessels.

Jesus commanded us in Matthew 10:7, "And *as* you go, preach." He did not say *if* you go! He said *when* you go! We need the strategy of Heaven to take this generation as Gideon took the Midianites. God told Gideon, "You shall defeat the Midianites as *one* man" (Judg. 6:16). That's strategy. That's warfare that will prevail! Let's go to Him for vision and then go to them with power! God is calling to a vanguard of men and women to lead this generation out of the cells of slavery and oppression. He wants us to understand the signs of the times and prepare their hearts for the time to come, just as Joseph prepared for the famine, storing up grain in the storehouses (see Gen. 42:48-49). These young lives are the eternal investment that will produce eternal rewards. The hearts of this generation are our modern-day storehouses.

Who will be a wise steward? Who will hear the Master's heart? Who will lay aside their personal agenda and set their affections on things above? This is the time of living sacrifices! Let hell smell the smoke of our bushels that are burning with the fire of passion and desire for His Kingdom come and His will be done! Now is the time for that kind of love! Now is the time for a cry of destiny!

CHAPTER 13

A SEASON OF SILENCE

But behold, you will be mute and not able to speak until the day these things take place, because you did not believe My words which will be fulfilled in their own time (Luke 1:20).

A season of silence has kept the Church in a place of immobility and sterility. She has stood on the fringes of the world like a spectator, waiting for a chance to enter the game. As Zechariah's mouth was silenced for a time, the Church's lips have been sealed for an appointed time when they would speak of a greater glory, a new revelation. "Until the days these things take place" was the timeline in Heaven, the starting gun to go off, setting the Church into harvest fields that are white and ripe.

The promise that kept the lips of Zechariah silent was of a child, a child who would "Give knowledge of salvation to His people" (see Luke 1:77). When Zechariah's mouth was opened, he not only prophesied of John the Baptist, but of the "*dayspring*," the Messiah—Jesus Christ, born of the virgin Mary. "My words which will be fulfilled in their own time" (Luke 1:20) had come upon them in the form of a Child that also signaled the start of an era of the Church, a revival of religion, and a reformation in the dry, dank halls of philosophy and law. It was a signpost that would mark the vast landscape of eternity forever.

Zechariah prophesied of a season of harvest and revival that would "give light to those who sit in darkness and the shadow of death, to guide our feet into the way of peace" (Luke 1:79). His season of silence had ended and a time of refreshing from the presence of the Lord had come. The lame would walk, the blind would see, and the dead would live again in this great season of revival. The reaper would now overtake the sower, and the immense harvest of captive humanity would hear the words of the "Way, the Truth, and the Life" (John 14:6).

In this day and hour we find the Church in a similar state of silence. She is unprepared, and sometimes even unwilling, to reach out into the dark waters of hopelessness and save a soul. This silence has made her mute to a world so desperate for her words. Zechariah's silence was imposed on him due to his sin of unbelief. He could not comprehend the thing that the angel had declared. He could not sound out the depths of its possibilities. He was stunned into silence and taken aback by the magnitude of what was promised.

Yet in the midst of his state of silence the promise still echoed in his mind and heart, "Until the days these things take place" (see Luke 1:20). A time was coming when the ground would shake and hardened humanity would cry out, "What must we do to be saved?" The veil would be violently torn, making way for the billions yet to be born. When this time arrived, all humankind would have the opportunity to "believe in their heart that God has raised Him from the dead, and be saved" (see Rom. 10:9). A season would arrive when the press would be so great that the roof would be torn from its place to get access to this great grace. Heaven would be in a state of explosive expansion from the billions that stood at her gates. Harvest was what Zechariah saw! A great harvest of souls! A great influx and spiritual awakening that would cause even the old saints to walk the streets again! Graves would be emptied and hearts would be filled with the glory of Almighty God.

The season of silence is coming to an end upon the face of the earth. The silence that has caused the Church to be a spectator instead of a participant on this great stage of life will soon be lifted. God will open the Church's lips as He opened Zechariah's, and we will declare a greater glory. We will tell of a greater revelation than is now known in rituals and routines. The lost will emerge from the shadows of this revelation with countenances that testify of a visitation. They will descend the mount of transfiguration with a revelation of Jesus Christ. The masses will hear and see the miracles done and the sound that they make, and billions will come to the knowledge of the Lord. The appointed time has come, the day of visitation is at hand—lift up your eyes! Your redemption draweth nigh! "Immediately his mouth was opened and his tongue loosed, and he spoke, praising God" (Luke 1:64).

Prophetic evangelists, who have sat in a state of mute silence for years, will be birthed from this season and will suddenly declare a glory and a power that has never been heard before. They will hear and speak things that will cause the world to fear the Lord again. Notice then in Zechariah's time as well, "Then fear came upon all who dwelt around them" (Luke 1:65). Churches will not be able to contain what is about to occur. No revival in history can reach the standard of what God is about to do in our midst. No book or article can define its greatness. But the fruit will be undeniable: *billions pressing into the Kingdom of God!* The heavens will suffer a violence never seen or to be seen again on this side of eternity. Get ready, Church! *The roof is about to be broken up!* The season of silence has ended. The season of glory has begun!

CHAPTER 14

ACTS OF
THE APOSTLES

Men who have hazarded their lives for the name of our Lord Jesus Christ (Acts 15:26).

The early Church was marked by two distinct attributes—power and boldness. It was comprised of men and women who hazarded their lives, their wealth, and their future for the gospel's sake. They were friends of the cross. The measuring stick of passion went deep into their hearts as they lived out this life of danger every waking hour. They weren't people who awoke to the Dow Jones and a cup of coffee! They turned their sheets down to the possibility of death and murder every sunrise! One step from their chambers held the chance of encountering a Roman sword, or worse, a cross.

Before someone can understand the power and grace that the early Church breathed, one must first comprehend the state they lived in. *Their circumstances demanded miracles!* They either experienced a miracle or they died. Signs and wonders weren't just trademarks or titles to best-selling books; they were the means of their survival! Unless God manifested, they died. In Acts 4:21, the religious leaders were forced to free them "because of the people, since they all glorified God for what had been done." Miracles weren't just a glitzy afterglow of their meetings; they were the difference between life and death for the apostles and the early Church.

It is no wonder that in Acts 4:29-30 (KJV) we find this early Church in solemn prayer: "And now Lord, behold their threatenings: and grant unto Thy servants, that with all *boldness* they may speak Thy word. *By stretching forth Thy hand to heal; and that signs and wonders may be done by the name of Thy holy child Jesus.*" Miracles weren't just an afterthought; they were unavoidable landmarks for the continued existence of these radical Christians on planet earth! Miracles were the salt that preserved them and the light that led them, and it was the very hand of God that defended them. One leader of the Jews put it this way, "And now I say to you, refrain from these men, and let them alone: for if this counsel or this work be of men, it will come to nought" (Acts 5:38, KJV). Two thousand years later that light still shines.

We *see* so few miracles today because we *need* so few. We have options; they didn't. We have a way out; they didn't. We have credit cards and debit cards; they certainly didn't. When we come to a place that we *need* a miracle, we'll *have* a miracle. With this in mind, I must then exhort you! In this hour of unprecedented violence and chaos, drugs and religion, and darkness and depravity, *we need miracles*! More than that, we need *miracle workers*! We need people who will walk in the same abandon to heavenly things as the early Church did, who will "hazard" everything for the sake of Christ. We must be a Church more concerned with the state of its city streets than the size of its offerings or building plans. Our hearts must be broken for the lives of the children who stand outside the church gates, mocking and jeering at the hypocrisy and inability to change even one heart, or heal one limb, or open one prison cell. You see, *when we truly need miracles, we will have miracles!* This generation is longing for the demonstration, not just the imitation, of His divine power and love. When we initiate, rather than imitate, His love, we'll see creative miracles that will rescue this shipwrecked generation from the shores of religion and powerlessness.

If only one attribute marked the early Church and her apostolic heart, it was compassion. She loved! She loved God! She loved her own! She loved a lost and dying world for which her Master had suffered in agony! She had witnessed that agony; it wasn't just a story. She'd *seen* the tears, the blood, and the wounds. It wasn't just an image on a canvas; it was reality. She had smelled the blood, tasted the salt in His tears, and thrust her hand in His side. She *knew* He was alive. In this state of mind, miracles were a common thing; they were as natural as breathing, eating, and sleeping. This was the life of a Church marked by compassion.

If there's anything that obstructs the free flow of miracles, signs, and wonders in the present-day Church, it's the lack of genuine compassion for the ones who *need* the miracles! How many times does Scripture tell us of Jesus' compassion? Over and over again, the Gospels tell us about the times that Jesus was moved with compassion toward the sick and the lost. It was the compassion of Jesus that instigated the miracles! He wasn't moved by necessity; He was moved by compassion.

Matthew 14:14 (KJV) defines the avenue of healing power and the miraculous: "And Jesus went forth, and saw a great multitude, and was moved with compassion toward them, and *He healed their sick.*" The acts of the apostles were marked by a divine love for God that moved them with divine compassion into the marketplaces where even human shadows had the capacity to heal. Not *all* shadows could impart the virtue to heal, only those who could answer the question, "Simon, do you love Me?" (see John 21:15).

If one other attribute marked the early Church, it was boldness. They were not afraid. They had nothing to be afraid of. For them, "to live was Christ and to die was gain" (see Phil. 1:21). They had faced their most terrible fears at Golgotha and they had died there. In the upper room, they were endowed with fearlessness, and they had an innate understanding of the grace of God, which enabled them to stand in front of the Jewish council and plead the gospel's case.

Today it overwhelms most Christians to stand in the local checkout stand at the grocery store and share a simple prayer or word of encouragement with a desperate mother, or come to the aid of a laid-off worker at the factory who will have to stand in the soup line this week to feed his family, or visit a 98-year-old widow who lies in her hospital bed and breathes her last.

Miracles will occur when the Church moves from fear to boldness and when it moves from the confines of the church building to the streets. It's in these places that we'll see the virtue leave the Body of Christ and go into the diseased and maimed. They are still reaching out; now it's up to us to boldly and fearlessly impart God's healing and life-changing message to them.

We are commanded to go to them: "Heal the sick, cleanse the lepers, raise the dead, cast out devils: *freely ye have received, freely give*" (Matt. 10:8, KJV).

We need apostolic succession to live as they lived, to act as they acted, to give like they gave, and to be poured out like they were poured out. To take that office we must be willing to live that life. To see their success we must first be willing to walk in their steps. The résumé of the apostle was not an easy one to fill. Let's walk a minute in their shoes and maybe it will help us understand their fruit. In Second Corinthians 6:1-10, we read the Apostles' Creed. Let's look at just a few of these attributes and then consider our own lives and what we're willing to lose and die to in order to see the same results.

- *"In stripes"*—They had offered their bodies up as living sacrifices to be beaten and bruised in order to see others saved and healed.

- *"In imprisonments"*—They were willing to lose freedom and liberties for what they proclaimed, counting all loss to gain the knowledge of Christ.

- *"In tumults"*—Wherever they walked, there were riots or revival; they understood nothing in-between.

- *"In labors"*—They expended every ounce of energy and strength to see His Kingdom on earth as it is in Heaven.

- *"In watchings"*—They knew what it meant to have sleepless nights in prayer and fasting.

- *"In fastings"*—They took literally the words, "deny yourself, take up your cross, and follow Me" (see Matt. 16:24).

This was the life of the apostolic Church. This will again be her mark in the coming days: selfless and powerful, losing everything to gain everything. It's the paradox of the cross.

The greatest challenges for the leadership in the Church today lie in training, not just entertaining, people. Leaders are instructed to train the Church "for the equipping of the saints, for the work of the ministry" (Eph. 4:12). It's not just to hold their attention; it's to teach them how to hold the tools and weapons that can win entire cities to Christ. It's not enough to tell them how to save a soul; they must be *shown* how to save a soul! The transition is from preaching to training. We need trainers, not just preachers. To speak and expound isn't enough; we need to show them how to fight the good fight. God is mobilizing an army. He's commissioning and appointing those who will "go before His face into every city and place where He Himself [is] about to go" (Luke 10:1).

Commissioning means: "Authority to act for another, authorizing certain duties or powers." Appoint means: "to set into office or decree, or to furnish or equip." God is appointing us as well as equipping us to go into the very place where He Himself desires to go with revival power and glory. The proof of revival is the absolute change of the moral climate over a city. When Philip was "appointed" and sent to Samaria, "there was great joy in that city" (Acts 8:8). Revival shakes the very foundation of a place and cries from the rooftops, "*Let My people go!*"

The idea of an "apostle" is more of an expression of the Father's heart than it is a person. It's the Father-heart of God demonstrated in human hearts. An apostle is more of a result of His love seen and experienced than it is a title or label. An apostolic age expresses a time and a season that the heart of the Father is expressing to the Church. Does that disqualify someone with the call and office of apostle? No. It's rather something seen instead of heard. It's a lifestyle more than it's a title. It's a power and passion rather than a name or occupation.

If you continue the discourse in Second Corinthians chapter 6, you'll find that apostles do not seek recognition, but rather maturation of those God has entrusted to them. Like their Master, they "[make themselves] of no reputation" (see Phil. 2:7). They are "unknown yet well-known" (see 2 Cor. 6:9). They seek not their own fanfare, but rather the welfare of others. They know the secret of contentment, learning "whatsoever state [they are in] therewith to be content" (see Phil. 4:11). This was an apostle. They possessed a human face that expressed the smile of God and a human hand that extended His grace and discipline. It was an attitude more than it was a man.

My prayer is this: God, give us an apostolic heart—a heart that is selfless and passionate for the things of God. Let us "suffer the loss of all things...and be found in Him, not having our own righteousness, which is of the law, but of Christ" (see Phil. 3:8-9). God, give us apostolic impact. Let's "turn the world upside down." Because of our abandon to You and the Cross, draw all men unto Yourself. Give us apostolic economy. "And all who believed were together, and had all things common; and sold their possessions and goods, and parted them to all men, as every man had need...Praising God, and having favour with all the people. *And the Lord added to the church daily such as should be saved*" (Acts 2:44-47, KJV).

This is an apostolic age and an apostolic Church, not just an apostolic person. Men categorize, but God is "no respecter of persons" (see Acts 10:34). This is an hour that we must count the cost and take up our cross and follow Him. In so doing we will walk in the steps of Christ Himself and see the fruit of His labors. We will take this message to the nations and make disciples of Christ, not of ourselves.

As quickly as we win them, we'll relinquish them into His hands. Our doctrine won't be "after man, but by the revelation of Jesus Christ" (Gal. 1:11-12). We will go in His power, not our own. In so doing we'll see apostolic results. "And with great power gave the apostles witness of the resurrection of the Lord Jesus: *and great grace was upon them all*" (Acts 4:33, KJV). Apostles were called to propagate a heavenly Kingdom, not an institution. God, give us apostles. God, give us all an apostolic heart. Give us the mind of Christ. "And has made us kings and priests to His God and Father, to Him be glory and dominion forever and ever. Amen" (Rev. 1:6).

CHAPTER 15

APOSTLES AND THE HARVEST

And they continued stedfastly in the apostles' doctrine and fellowship, and in breaking of bread, and in prayers. And fear came upon every soul: and many wonders and signs were done by the apostles. And all that believed were together, and had all things common; And sold their possessions and goods, and parted them to all men, as every man had need. And they, continuing daily with one accord in the temple, and breaking bread from house to house, did eat their meat with gladness and singleness of heart, Praising God, and having favour with all the people. And the Lord added to the church daily such as should be saved (Acts 2:42-47, KJV).

Apostolic times in reference to the New Testament era equated to souls and harvest. A foundation was built that could withstand the weight of glory that God was pouring out onto it. A foundation was constructed that could sustain and hold the masses that were about to stand on it—the Church. "And with great power gave the apostles witness of the resurrection of the Lord Jesus: and great grace was upon them all" (Acts 4:33, KJV). Power evangelism was the hallmark of the early apostolic ministry. It was the power to overwhelm the popular opinion that Jesus was dead and reveal to them a resurrected Christ. Paul summed up the apostolic message in two sentences, "For I delivered unto you first of all that which I also received, how that Christ died for our sins according to the scriptures; and that He was buried, and that He rose again the third day according to the scriptures" (1 Cor. 15:3-4, KJV).

Many books have been written on the apostolic but I believe a key element is missing from most of them: harvest. God gave the world apostles to set them free and deliver to them the message of salvation and revelation of Christ. Paul again defined the apostolic passion in Romans 15:19-20 (KJV), which states: "Through mighty signs and wonders, by the power of the Spirit of God; so that from Jerusalem, and round about unto Illyricum, I have fully preached the gospel of Christ. Yea, so have I strived to preach the gospel, not where Christ was named, lest I should build upon another man's foundation." Paul's passion was to go where Christ had not been preached and to build as God had built—from nothing. A breed of apostolic ministers is being anointed in this hour to "go where no man has gone before." They will blaze a trail of revival through untapped areas that have not fully heard the gospel of Jesus Christ. Many have heard about Jesus in some form and fashion, but they have not fully heard the gospel of Jesus Christ.

A classic example of this is the Native Americans. They have heard a message of Jesus, but they are yet to be presented, by and large, with the full gospel message of Jesus Christ. They have received a "white, Anglo-Saxon" version of the gospel. Many have yet to see the Jesus that Paul had known. They have seen an English version of Jesus painted on the ceilings of cathedral walls, but they have not seen a resurrected Jesus who is full of glory and might. They have not been told about the Jesus who does not look at the outward man but seeks for those after His own heart. After 200 years of evangelizing, Native America remains predominately untouched by His glory and grace. Almost purposely by the modern-day church, Native America is ignored and seen as a missionary endeavor rather than a hidden army waiting to be awakened.

Indigenous people and tribes around the globe are waiting desperately for a true apostolic message full of power and truth. An army of apostolic people is coming on the scene right now that will defy modern versions and interpretations of how ministry is done, how it is dressed, how it acts, and how it should be promoted. These soldiers are going to take the message of His resurrection to the uttermost parts of the earth with signs and wonders following. Web pages and magazines will not be able to keep up with their exploits and miracles. Only Heaven will be able to record their comings and goings.

God wants to see apostles at work as they were in Acts 5:12-15 (KJV):

> *And by the hands of the apostles were many signs and wonders wrought among the people; (and they were all with one accord in Solomon's porch. And of the rest durst no man join himself to them: but the people magnified them. And believers were the more added to the Lord, multitudes both of men and women.) Insomuch that they brought forth the sick into the streets, and laid them on beds and couches, that at the least the shadow of Peter passing by might overshadow some of them.*

The apostolic power cannot be contained in upper rooms and confined places. Whenever anyone tried to put apostles behind four walls, God sent earthquakes and angels to get them out! We see this truth in Acts 5:18-20 (KJV): "And [they] laid their hands on the apostles, and put them in the common prison. But the angel of the Lord by night opened the prison doors, and brought them forth, and said, Go, stand and speak in the temple to the people all the words of this life." True apostolic power cannot be defined in books and conferences; it is defined by city-wide transformation and revival. The new converts and souls are the pages of apostles' books written on the fleshly tablets of human hearts. The exploits of their children write their biographies and repertoires. Nations and un-reached people groups are their glory and aspiration. Nothing else will satisfy them. They cannot rest easy when there are still foundations to be built to withstand more of His glory stored up for the earth. They are master builders ever striving for the upward call in Christ Jesus. They quickly forget the former glory and past victories; they are always looking for new, fresh blood. Such is the life of the apostle.

The echo of Christ's command to the New Testament apostles still stands today. "And He said unto them, Go ye into all the world, and preach the gospel to every creature" (Mark 16:15, KJV). This is unavoidable and without need of interpretation. The simplicity of Jesus' command rings true here: GO! A "going" involves being injected into the heart of God's people. Like the apostles of old, today's apostles will be driven to go "not where Christ was named" (Rom. 15:20, KJV) but where hearts still yearn to know the good news of Jesus Christ.

"And a vision appeared to Paul in the night; there stood a man of Macedonia, and prayed him, saying, Come over into Macedonia, and help us. And after he had seen the vision, immediately we endeavoured to go into Macedonia, assuredly gathering that the Lord had called us for to preach the gospel unto them" (Acts 16:9-10, KJV). A Macedonian call is resounding through the Church in this hour. We are seeing a vision from Heaven of people desperate for His grace and salvation. The Macedonian call now for the modern-day Church is our streets and cities, the highways and byways, the dark places that have been predominately void of a witness of Jesus. This is the direction in which the apostolic will direct us. As it was 2,000 years ago, so it will be now.

Division must be put aside. "But the multitude of the city was divided: and part held with the Jews, and part with the apostles" (Acts 14: 4, KJV). I believe that the division in God's camp right now and in the future will be between those who desire to sit back and not participate in the harvest and those who posture themselves to receive it. Churches will be known simply by whether they are receptive to the harvest in all of its diverse color or whether they are not. There will be no neutral ground. Time is too short.

"And the apostles said unto the Lord, Increase our faith" (Luke 17:5, KJV). The prayer of the apostolic in this hour will be for more faith. We must have faith to reach the unreached people groups, faith to mobilize this army of soul winners, and faith to remove the mountains of tradition and religion that stand in the way of true revival. God will grant their request and give them the power again to move whole cities into the Kingdom of God with their end-time message and gospel.

CHAPTER 16

THE NEW BREED

As we face yet another millennia with its epic challenges and climatic changes, the thought that our contemporary methods are sufficient to reach the world around us leaves us with an uneasy feeling of insufficiency. A vacuum has been created in the hearts of this generation by the failure of modern religious icons. The youth now turn to false facades created by computers and imagery, which leave our ancient encryptions of God archaic. The Church as they see it is no longer relevant. Anything that means something to them we call unholy, thus widening the margin of misunderstanding.

Echoing Paul, who became all things to all men, we need to immerse ourselves into their present culture and lifestyle, their music and movies, and their rhythm and rhyme in order to discover the pulse and passion of their hearts. Modern theology promotes a different message of judging and condemning these expressions and images, which only prolongs their inherent destiny. Our socially and culturally shaped religion leaves no room for diversity or creativity. We produce black and white pictures of Jesus as the world promotes a panoramic picture of a new age. Our religious adherence to tradition reinforces their view of our irrelevance.

Their modern prophets rap rather than preach. They sing rather than teach. They graphically express their hearts and feelings while the Church is shrouded behind socially and religiously correct doctrine, afraid to come out and touch the world around them. Christians have literally created a secret society of T-shirts, slogans, and bumper stickers. Our identity is wrapped up in current Christian trends and books rather than God's awesome love for the people living around us. We have created a fairy-tale landscape where the world is not welcome.

Almost everything we do in church is geared and focused on the saved rather than the lost or unsaved. We have reversed the cycle of reform created in the first-century Church, which when "scattered abroad went everywhere preaching the gospel" (see Acts 8:4), and have become an introverted personality defined by a building or a denomination. We have built a mansion rather than a manger. The world is still looking for Jesus in the simplicity of everyday life as the shepherds once did in Bethlehem. Today they are confronted with an intricate structure based on bylaws and statements of faith rather than the power and glory of God. We are in a present state of "Ichabod" in the American church and her para-church ministries.

Under the surface, though, a reformation is brewing. The hearts of the masses are not satisfied with the modern trends of tradition. They cannot conform to the scheduled meetings of Sunday and Wednesday, which emphasize a sophisticated softness rather than His suffering, prestige instead of power, and position over purpose. A radical reformation is on the horizon of Christendom. The fires of revolution are kindled in the bosom of millions. They will not settle for the mundane, lazy, relaxed stance of modern leadership that is so afraid of change and prefers the predictable rather than the radical. Those days are coming to an end.

Unfortunately, God is being defined today by sharply dressed orators who have distanced themselves from the world they were sent to liberate. Somehow, they have evolved past the simplicity presented by Christ in His mission to reach the world 2,000 years ago. The contradiction is dramatic as we glimpse in the gospel the lifestyle of Jesus and His followers. At every turn they were reaching out and touching the broken-down vehicles of humanity around them. They forfeited their own needs to meet the hunger of the masses around them. Times have changed. Mountains of self-help books tell us how we can improve. The gospel of Jesus is shockingly different—He tells you to die, to deny yourself, and take up your cross. Jesus' message is a lifestyle of self-sacrifice rather than of self-improvement. I see a cloud of reformation forming over the land. In the days to come, religious peer pressure will not be able to hold back the numbers who will go up the mountain of the Lord, leaving behind the institutional relics of man-made myth. My friend, this revolution has begun.

There is a metamorphosis in the contemporary landscape called ministry. The face that it presents to the world is drastically changing. The era of refined and religiously defined personalities is over. A new breed of unorthodox, nontraditional rule-breakers is emerging on the stage of the theologically correct. They are tearing down the walls of cold, unattended altars and making way for a world desperate for a spiritual reality. They are not afraid to embrace their own humanity and present a God who is reachable and tangible. They refuse to conform to the guillotine of dispensational thinking. They are a reformational generation, not only by principle, but also by action. Their works speak much louder than words. They demonstrate a living Christ in a world of idols. They are preparing the way of the Lord in a social, economical, evolving world. You will see them in the back-lots of movie sets, on MTV, and even in the corporate offices of the humanistic elite. They are not afraid of the lions of commercialism and compromise. They will be the Daniels in the dens of corporate empires. They cannot be bought.

Their faces are etched with the lines of destiny. Their hearts burn with an anxiousness to see His will truly accomplished in the world around them. They are fearless and relentless. They are not only history-makers, they are also future-tellers and seers who peer past the torn veil of the temporal. They defy mindsets that conform to a previous experience of faith, and they make a vow of sacrifice that will rival the martyrs of Hebrews chapter 11. They set the trends that will change the tide of a generation from the hypnotic sounds of satan to the prophetic shores of His love and power. They will part the red sea of modern intellectualism and allow a people to cross over to dry land. They will leap the wall of liberalism and conservatism and show the world the heart of God.

They are the new breed. They are the lover-warriors of Solomon, who carry the couch of the King in war. They are not afraid of spiritual intimacy, neither are they afraid to engage the enemy. Their exploits will be greater than those of David's mighty men, for they will be the ones who carry the Messiah into the nations. Unlike their predecessors, they will have the blueprints for the tabernacle of David and will set their hands to its completion. All nations will flow into it. This new breed will know what it means to build a tabernacle. They will follow the pillar of fire by night and the cloud of smoke by day. They will go on to know the Lord. They will upset the tables of preplanning and bring forth the spontaneity of revival. They will leap the barriers of conference registration tables and prepare the way of the Lord. Reformation is knocking at the Church door.

Like Martin Luther in 15th-century Germany, they will come with a thesis of revival in their DNA. Some will be labeled heretical and crazy. Others will be called the devil and beelze-bub; but, like their Master Jesus, they will "pass through them" to carry the love of the gospel to other cities. For this reason they were created. For this season were they made. A great wave of religious persecution is about to purge this new breed, breaking away any pretense and self-will. Like the three boys in the fiery furnace, they will come from the flames of envy and strife unscathed. They will emerge from the desert of exile with a word from the Lord. They will decree a new thing that has not been taught or heard before in the halls of modern methodology.

Open fields and marketplaces will be their proving ground. They will be forged by harvest and proved by revival. They will flee the confinement of the upper room to manifest a resur-rected Christ. They will refuse to eat the leaven of the Pharisees. They will eat the bread of simplicity, thus producing His author-ity. They are reformers and lovers. They will be the ink of histo-ry that carries His posterity. They will set a standard of love that is unavoidable and undeniable. The earth and the fullness thereof will flow into it. The walls of indifference and religion will fall flat as they circle the cities with His love and authority. Whole metropolitan Mecca's will melt under the intense mani-festation of liberty they bring. Entire cities will be saved. This is the future; this is our hope. Let the revolution begin! Let this new breed take center stage.

CHAPTER 17

CHRIST IN HIS DISTRESSING DISGUISE

Mother Teresa once said:

I do not agree with the big way of doing things. To us what matters is an individual. If we wait to get the numbers, we will be lost in the numbers. I believe in person to person; every person is Christ for me, and since there is only one Jesus, that person is only one person in the world for me at that moment.

In a world full of fantasy and fiction, it's sometimes difficult to discover the face of God in such a maze of humanity. In the fancy disguise of religion, it's sometimes even harder. In the face of piety one can get lost in duty and ritual, somehow forgetting compassion. We never hear the beat of an orphan's heart through the rapturous sounds of religion. We never see the sinner's hungry stares through the stained-glass windows of our cathedrals. We have become deaf to the drowning masses as they slip past by the millions and millions into an uncertain eternity. God forbid that the epitaph of this generation would read, "The harvest is past, the summer is ended, and we are not saved" (Jer. 8:20, KJV).

The harvest is white as we stare into the vast expanse of a new millennium. But the laborers are still few. The paradox is still as perplexing as it was when Christ walked the earth 2,000 years ago. It's a simple message of love and charity, yet it's forgotten in the clamor of human achievement and selfishness. *We pass Him by every day as we strive for spiritual experience.* He's left on the streets, surprised and rejected. The words of John 1:11 are still true: "He came to His own, and His own did not receive Him."

Never in history have we stood at such a precipice of possibility. Masses of souls stare at the Church as they did in Acts 3:5 (KJV): "And gave heed to them, expecting to receive something from them." What will we give to them this hour? Can we say, "Silver and gold have I none, but what I have I give to you"? Or will we continue to offer wealth and prosperity without wholeness and posterity? Can we demonstrate the power without the pressure? The passion without a price? Prophecy without a price tag? Oh, that we could see what Paul saw when he exclaimed: "For though I preach the gospel, I have nothing to glory of: for necessity is laid upon me; yea, woe is unto me, if I preach not the gospel" (1 Cor. 9:16, KJV). And again, "What is my reward then? That when I preach the gospel, I may present the gospel of Christ without charge, that I may not abuse my authority in the gospel" (1 Cor. 9:18). When you hear this message from the pulpit, the gates of hell will not prevail.

The faces of a thousand broken hearts stare at us every day with outstretched hands, waiting at the corner for Jesus to pass by. They've been waiting for a long time. Many have spent all of their living on doctors, but to no avail. Still they wait. They wait for the living Christ to be loosed from the bondage of human hearts and expressed to an expectant world. They're waiting for us, His Church. As Jesus hides behind the strain and scars of the masses, He cries: "I will rise now...and go about the city; in the streets and in the squares I will seek the one I love" (Song of Sol. 3:2). He's not hard to find. You can see Him plainly in the eyes of a child and in the eyes of an old man as he stumbles aimlessly down the street. You can see Him in the eyes of a mother, alone and struggling. You can find Him if you really desire Him. He's waiting; He's watching, waiting and watching for His Bride. "Let the bridegroom go forth of His chamber, and the bride out of her closet" (Joel 2:16, KJV).

In the streets of America one doesn't have to go far to see distressed faces. They leer at you from the corner. They stare at you from car windows. A generation of restless hearts is silhouetted on the backdrop of life, hungry and desperate. People are desperate for the reality of Jesus demonstrated unconditionally through earthen vessels to free them from guilt and condemnation. They are desperate for a hand of help to dare to reach from the Church's shores and to cast a line of life to the ocean of hapless humanity. *This generation of youths is the fuel waiting for the flame of destiny to ignite their hearts with holy passion.* They stand idly on the corners and when asked why, they reply, "No one has hired us" (Matt. 20:6-7). They say, "No one has given us a chance! No one has seen the worth and the value in us. No one will give place to the glory of God in us." Jesus' response is: "Let the little children come to Me and do not forbid them, for of such is the kingdom of heaven" (Matt. 19:14).

God stares at us from their haunting eyes, waiting for and imploring the Church to rise to her feet and declare from the housetops, "*But you are a chosen generation*" (1 Pet. 2:9)! If there's a prophetic sound in the land, it's one of restoration not desolation. God is looking for those who will: "Build the old wastes, they shall raise up the former desolations, and they shall repair the waste cities, the desolations of many generations"

(Isa. 61:4, KJV). If there's any anointed in this day they'll not condemn and slander, but rather, "Bind up the broken-hearted...proclaim liberty to the captives, and the opening of the prison to them that are bound" (Isa. 61:1, KJV). God isn't looking for judges; He's looking for lions who will roar His love into the hearts of a billion broken people.

What we need to do is make room for the lost, not just through programs, but through people getting involved with the everyday hurts of their city. They must get involved, not from a safe distance, but directly. They must be a bridge between the Church and the street, as Philip was between Jerusalem and Samaria. *We have to stand in the gap!*

The word translated as *hedge* in Luke 14:23 comes from the Greek word meaning "pit" or "prison." The word *compel* is derived from the Greek words that mean, "to drag or dredge up as if in a net." When Jesus commanded His servants to "go into the highways and hedges and compel them to come in" (see Luke 14:23), what He was really saying was, "Go out into the pits and prisons of society and cast the net of My love into the cesspool of moral depravity and bring them in! Translate them from darkness into My Kingdom!"

We need more than just yearly food drives! What do they eat the rest of the year? Our churches need to become the "storehouses" they were intended to be. The misinterpretation of Scripture in Malachi, which preaches a formula of prosperity rather than charity, has brought the Church into a place of spiritual poverty. Doors that should be open 24 hours a day are locked and barred while the lost wander aimlessly and blindly in the local tavern. We need teams that will stay at churches during the night to receive the least of them. In ancient Israel the watchmen weren't on furlough after midnight, but today we are fast asleep. Their watch had only begun! We need outreaches from every suburban church into the inner city. We need "nets" that are cast out into the deep to dredge the alleys for children molested and forgotten. We need outreaches that keep the light of salvation on all night, offering coffee, a pastry, and a prayer.

The world needs the Church to stir herself from the comfort of indifference. The Church needs her leaders and pastors to be the first to step from the pulpit to the street. Jesus didn't live behind the safety of veiled synagogue walls! NO! He moved among the common man! He walked with them every day! He ate in their houses and healed their bodies! Where in church history did we transcend from the marketplace to the monastery?

The secret of church growth isn't accountants and building programs. NO! It's charity and evangelism! It's a passion for souls and a compassion for the lost! It's the courage to step from the confines of religion and boldly invade the darkness and declare, "I am the light of the world! I am the salt of the earth!" Then and only then will we "hasten the coming of the day of God" (see 2 Pet. 3:12).

"JESUS STILL BLEEDS"

Every day they stare at you from their mansions on the streets,
The homeless and destitute, hungry and begging for something to eat.
Blank stares and hollow eyes just seem to look right through you,
As you hastily pass them by not knowing what to say or do,
Love is compromised...

You can see her every night, restless, on Fourth and Main,
It's so obvious the scars, bruised and filled with the past's pain.
She shifts her eyes from the world and stumbles on down the road,
Aimless and abandoned with nowhere left to go,
She slowly dies...

The little boy's face is so dirty,
He couldn't be more than four.
As the church walks by, all of Heaven now implores,
"Reach out! Reach out! Reach out!
Show them that someone cares!
In all of your religion and revelation,
Let them know that Jesus is there!
To heal them, to love them, and to make them whole,
I tell you now, My church, I command you,
LET THE WORLD KNOW!"

The prisoner paces, restless and confused,
In an eight-by-ten box, rejected and abused.
Tattoos parade up and down his arms,
Reminding him of the mistakes that left the scars.
"But when I was in prison, why didn't you visit Me?
Why did you leave Me alone to bleed?"

The widow lies there staring from her room,
Unable to walk, unable to move.
Praying that someone would come to ease the pain,
Hoping and praying for a friendly face.
"Pure religion and undefiled is this,
To visit the widow and the orphan in their distress."

Even today Jesus still bleeds,

Crying out to you and me,

"GO! GO! GO!
SET THE CAPTIVES FREE!"
When will the Church finally see,
That when they do it to them,
They are really doing it to Me?
When will they realize,
That religion is a cheap disguise,
For the children who are left to die.

They have to see them through their Father's eyes.
Love no longer compromised...

Today I saw Jesus
In an old woman's eyes.
I saw the glory of the Father
In the widow and the despised,
And I suddenly realized,
Why He died...

The old woman looked at me and said,
"No one has visited me in so many years,
No one has ever considered my pain and my tears.
But what you've said today, I will never forget,
The price a Man paid for my sin and my debt..."

Jesus still bleeds for the least of these...

CHAPTER 18

JESUS
COMMANDS US TO GO!

In the days of Paul and Peter, "go ye into all the world" wasn't an option or a semi-retirement plan once their own pursuits were dried up. It was their life, their passion. "To live was Christ and to die was gain" (see Phil. 1:21). There were very few options at this level of commitment. It was all or nothing. They had signed on the dotted line of self-sacrifice. They had put their hand to the plow, and they knew what it meant to be "fit for the Kingdom of God." When they walked away from family and career to follow the Nazarene, they knew there was no turning back. They'd gone through the veil of selfishness and entered the realm of selflessness. They had put on Christ.

They were missionaries; they were "ambassadors of Christ." They were sent ones, apostles, disciples. They knew only two words: "Follow Me." Their creed echoed the words of Christ: "Deny yourself, and take up your cross" (see Matt. 16:24). There was no multiple choice. They had counted the cost and the conclusion was simple: *everything*. It was no longer "I" who lived; it was Christ only, "and the life they now lived in the flesh they lived unto the Son of God who had died for them" (see Gal. 2:20). In their mortal bodies abided the Spirit who had raised Him from the dead; they couldn't be stopped. "Persecuted, but not forsaken; cast down, but not destroyed" (2 Cor. 4:9, KJV). The fire of their passion couldn't be quenched; death would only stoke the flames of their message. They couldn't be bought, and, when threatened, they prayed; and the place where they stood was shaken.

Today the level of commitment goes no farther than the church doors. The cries of salvation are rarely heard in the marketplaces anymore. We have boxed it up and packaged it in pretty paper. It has a "form of godliness, but denies the power" (see 2 Tim. 3:5) from whence it came. Pentecost has become perfumed instead of seasoned with fire. The acts of the apostles have been reassembled to appear to be a performance rather than His power to save and set free from the grip of sin and hell. The sinner continues on his perilous journey while the Church has prematurely abandoned the altars of repentance and salvation. We preach wealth as the world dies in unparalleled poverty and misery. The world cries out for Jesus as we busy ourselves with pleasure and selfish pursuits. The masses march to the sound of church bells that never sound the alarm of death and hell.

My prayer is: God, give us a New Testament Church once again! Give us a place where the preacher cries for souls more than he pleads for money! Where the prophets no longer "prophesy for hire" (see Mic. 3:11) but desire only to see His Bride rise in awesome signs and wonders to usher in this great harvest of souls! Remove, if you must, this monopoly of ministries that hoards the wealth that You meant for missions. Take away the buildings of those who build their own kingdoms while ignoring Yours. Tear down these lofty towers of pride that reach and reach and never touch the streets with Your compassion—towers that have become willingly ignorant of Your words, "Go ye into all the world and preach the gospel to every creature" (Mark 16:15, KJV).

Forgive us for our selfish ambition that overlooks the publican and the harlot, seeking instead the rich and wealthy. O Lord, we are backslidden! We have forgotten Your commandments! We've left our first love. We've ceased to do the first works! We've forgotten that You hide Yourself in the faces of the "least of our brethren," that when we touch them, we also touch You. Lord, open our eyes to the world around us. Open our hearts to the ones who lie wasted and emaciated, begging for alms at the city gate. Let us offer not only our money, but also the power of Your Spirit to say to them, *"Rise up and walk!"* O Lord, restore to Your ministers a passion for prayer so that they will emerge with a message for these last days. Let us come down from the Mount of Transfiguration with a revelation of Jesus Christ. *O Lord, set us free from the ocean of red tape that drowns Your Church in legalism and traditionalism. Free us from that sin that so easily besets us called religion, pious but powerless religion.*

God has called us to be His ambassadors, His missionaries! God forbid we stand before Him someday with the same excuses they did when they were invited to the wedding feast! "I have married a wife!" "I must tend to my field!" "I have bought five yoke of oxen!" Only the words of Paul will give entrance into Heaven! "I have fought a good fight, I have finished my course, I have kept the faith" (2 Tim. 4:7, KJV).

The résumé of the apostles didn't consist of seminaries or degrees, but rather scourging and beatings, rods and stoning. They were men and women who had "suffered the loss of all things that they could gain Christ" (Phil. 3:8). Ministry wasn't a form of gain or prosperity, but suffering and long nights in the deep! They "carried the scars of Christ" (see Col. 1:24). They knew what it meant to "be abased and to abound" (Phil. 4:12).

They had gained the wisdom of their Master, "in whatever state I am in, to be content" (see Phil. 4:11). They were slaves of grace, chained to Christ. God, give us a thousand times a thousand of such saints! Give us saints marked by Your love and grace, who have come from the mount and have seen Your face and who are determined to finish this race!

A vanguard of men, women, and children is rising from the shadows to storm the earth with God's love and power! Escaping from the confines of religion and tradition, they will give their lives in the fields that are so white and heavy with souls. In the coming days, many of His children will take their families, losing friends and home, never to be seen again this side of Heaven, and be poured out as a drink offering for their Lord. He will send them Himself. The only ordination they'll carry is His Holy Spirit. Their only validation will be His power. They will echo the words of Paul, "But I certify you, brethren, that the gospel which was preached of me is not after man. For I neither received it of man, neither was I taught it, *but by the revelation of Jesus Christ*" (Gal. 1:10-12, KJV).

They will stand in front of skeptics with the words of Isaiah, "The Spirit of the Lord God is upon me; because *the Lord has anointed me to preach* good tidings to the poor, *He has sent me* to bind up the brokenhearted, to proclaim liberty to the captives, and the opening of the prison to them that are bound" (Isa. 61:1). They may be cast out, but they will in no way be forgotten. They may be despised and rejected now, but in eternity their words and deeds will be recorded.

A greater requirement is coming upon the Church in this hour. All of our resources—land, buildings, and wealth—will be for the saving of souls and the reaching of nations. An introverted Church will become an open door of provision and power. Time is too short to "build bigger barns." There is no retirement for the saint of God! Our calling is to be "offered up as a living sacrifice, broken and contrite, which the Lord will not despise" (see Rom. 12:1 and Ps. 51:17). These are the days He's calling for missionaries, ambassadors, preachers, and teachers to take His power to the ends of the earth. *Jesus still commands us to go!*

"HERE AM I, SEND ME"

O Lord, here am I, send me;
I offer up my life as a drink offering,
Like David, to be poured out like water,
To desire nothing but the will of My Father.

O Lord, here am I, send me,
To help those in darkness, finally see.
To set the captives free,
Grant pardon to those in captivity.

O Lord, here am I, send me;
I pledge my head to Heaven,
To the lowly help me condescend,
To the poor I will be a friend.

Here am I, send me!
I will go when others flee!
To the alleys and the streets!
O Lord! Here am I! Send me!

CHAPTER 19

TODAY IS THE
DAY OF SALVATION

And on some have compassion, making a difference: And others save with fear, pulling them out of the fire (Jude 1:22-23, KJV).

If we were walking down the street tonight and saw a little girl dangling from a second-story window, smoke billowing from the cracks around her, flames shooting from the roof as her screams pierced the night air, would we hesitate to intervene? Would we pause and think and contemplate if it was "the right thing to do?" Or would we instead leap and run to her aid, doing whatever humanly possible to see her rescued? It doesn't take much meditation to answer these questions. What if it were your own child in that burning house? What would your reaction be then? How swiftly and fearlessly would you risk life and limb to see her saved?

Now think about this. All around us there are lost and desperate children littering our city streets. Millions mill about and wander this nation's metropolises. They are homeless, fatherless, and terrified. You see them at the bus stops, shopping malls, and street corners. But when do you see them outside the church perimeters, in the foyer, or in the parking lot, hoping to get in? When do you see them filling our Sunday morning services, pressing forward to reach the altar? I must ask, where is the army of lost and lonely children who march this nation's streets? What have we done in all of our conferences and convocations to reach them? How long will we continue to build larger enterprises and ministries as these little ones perish and go to hell? I think the Father is asking us the same thing today: "Suffer the little children to come unto Me" (see Luke 18:16).

Once I heard a story of a man who was driving downtown in a large city when he saw a young girl on the corner scantily dressed and cold. She paced back and forth, vulnerable and scared. The man went home that night and cried out to the Lord in frustration, "Lord! What have You done to help these children? What have You done? What will You do?" There was no response. Later that night the Lord suddenly answered his persistent prayer: "I have done something about it—*I made you.*"

God created us as His vessels of mercy. We are to be His ships of grace, sailing into this world to deliver His salvation. If we lift Him up, He will draw everyone to Him. But first we must lift Him up! First we must enter the ocean of humanity and cast a rope of rescue. We can't expect the drowning masses to somehow reach our harbors and docks; we must launch out into the deep and throw out the nets! Fishing isn't done from the safe shores of church; it's done in the dangerous depths of the world! Out in the deep is where we take in a great catch. Out in the deep is where we see His miracles. We've played the entertainer, entertaining the crowds of Christians to get a good offering. We've sold our wares and paraded our gifts, oblivious to the desperate cries all around us.

Jesus said, "Follow Me and I will make you fishers of men" (Matt. 4:19). Not, "Follow Me and I will make you a great and mighty prophet who all the earth reveres." I believe the test to all of our prophecy and revelation is the impact it has on a dying planet. What impression does it make on the hearts of lost humanity? What impact does it have on heathen nations? God, burn up the wood, hay, and stubble of human effort. Consume the worthless work of man's hand. Give us revivalists who burn for the lost as You did and who lose sleep and fortune to see even one saved. Give us people who dream and wake to Your burning desire to see this world saved. God is "not willing that any should perish but that all should come to repentance" (2 Pet. 3:9).

Somehow we've allowed the spirit of indifference to set up camp in our midst. We're indifferent to the world around us. We can pray, but we can't reach out. We can talk about soul-winning and have conferences about soul-winning, but when are we really winning souls? If you or I were asked, "When is the last time you personally led a soul to Jesus and watched him become born again?" what would we honestly answer? What's your answer now? "Well, that isn't my calling! God hasn't told me to do that." This is the root of the deception that has crept unaware into our hearts and churches. Somehow that deception has made us forget the great command of Jesus to every believer, "Go into all the world and preach the gospel to every creature" (see Matt. 28:19).

We stand by on the sidelines of human demise and speak our messages, sing our songs, prophesy, and preach, and all the while we never reach even one lost soul. Let the words of Christ burn in our consciences: "Which man of you, having a hundred sheep, if he loses one of them, does not leave the ninety-nine in the wilderness, and go after the one which is lost until he finds it" (Luke 15:4).

William Booth, founder of the Salvation Army, was once heard saying, "I wish I could dangle every convert over hell for 30 minutes so they could know what they were saving people from!" It seems we've lost all concept of hell and eternity. Like the rich man, we're startled that there's such a place and beg for our family not to suffer such a state. Or like the Pharisee, we can purposely ignore the eternal judgment waiting for every soul not washed in the blood of Jesus. This eventually numbs our conscience and relieves us of any urgency and compassion for the lost. We can prophesy ourselves right out of any effectiveness and impact on a human soul. We become prophets of fallacy, never reaching where it's needed most—the world.

I must shout from the housetops! The endless books of revelation, the current prophetic buzz, the endless conferences and meetings, what are they doing to change the moral and spiritual climate in our cities? Are souls being won into the Kingdom of God? Are we baptizing new converts and experiencing explosive expansion in Heaven? Are the violent gangs being curbed and changed because of the things we're doing? If not, we are failing. We have no fruit that remains, and we must seriously and severely examine our hearts and return to our first love and first works. We must renovate our churches and position ourselves for harvest. We have to open doors opened only for church attendees, yet shut to the lost and dying. We must cater to the lost sheep, not to our own selfish enterprises. God, give us a heart aflame with Your love and passion! Give us a heart that weeps as You wept over Your city, that it would not miss its day of visitation, its salvation. Remind all of us, Lord, that *today is the day of salvation!*

CHAPTER 20

FROM CONFERENCE TO CONFRONTATION

Once a year, William Booth would gather the Salvation Army missionaries and workers in England to strategize and pray about how to more effectively affect unreached areas for Jesus Christ. People would flood the altars everywhere they went. Testimonies abounded that on occasion the power of God was so wonderfully manifest in the meetings that people would be frequently struck down, overwhelmed with a sense of the presence and power of God.

Their fervency for the gospel knew no bounds. They would then march through the streets, beating hand-held drums, waving banners, and passing out handbills for their nightly revival meetings. Sometimes beaten and bruised, they'd assemble, and the fire of God would fall as souls were saved. General Booth's battle cry was: "Go for souls and go for the worst." The worst of sinners was saved, saloons were closed, and entire cities were shaken. At another time, two Salvation Army workers set out to found a new work, only to meet with failure and opposition. Frustrated and tired, they appealed to Booth to close the rescue mission. General Booth sent back a telegram with two words on it: "Try tears." They followed his advice and witnessed mighty revival. When spit on during the Midlands tour, Booth encouraged his fellow soldiers, "Don't rub it off—it's a medal!"

God is putting the fire of self-sacrifice back into our hearts to preach the gospel with passion and fervency. Katherine Booth was once heard saying, "At least let them see the tears in your eyes when you tell them about the Master's love." God is giving us tears again—tears of compassion and tears of passion for the lost and perishing who flood our streets and cities. We must be a "Salvation Army" once again, beating the drum of the Father's heart through the streets of this country.

Revival is only a direct manifestation of the burning love of Jesus displayed in human hands and hearts. It's only an overflow of a Church ablaze with the fervent passion of Jesus Christ—a passion that compelled Him past mobs and whips to hang on a tree. Once we are lit with this kind of love, we'll see revival and harvest! *Let's burn, then! Let's burn!*

Later in William Booth's ministry he came to the conclusion that the conference was no longer necessary; the formal gathering that began to produce nothing but more formality was turning into a dead tradition. He said later:

> There have been more than enough conferences, and congresses, and committees, and deliberations. It is time to ACT! There is not a moment to lose! There cannot be any question to what we have to do. No more conferences! No more doubt! No more delay! Arise, ye children of the light, and buckle on the armor bright, and now prepare yourselves to fight, against the world and satan. We are called to be saints. We are called to be brothers and sisters of Jesus, to fight with Him, for

Him, with every particle of strength we have to the last grasp. That is enough! No more conference!

Again the Lord is pressing on the hearts of His leaders and ministers to take "conference" to a completely different level. *From conference to confrontation*, the Church must march from the upper-room experience into the marketplaces of every city, heralding a harvest and reformation. What's being reported in churches as revival and renewal will be eclipsed by the awesome demonstration of what God is about to do on the streets. Like in the first-century Church, these things will be common occurrences: "So that they brought the sick *out into the streets* and laid them on beds and couches, that at least the shadow of Peter passing by might fall on some of them. Also a multitude gathered from the surrounding cities to Jerusalem, bringing sick people and those tormented by unclean spirits, and they were all healed" (Acts 5:15-16).

Revival will demand unity. In the normal church pace of program and predictability one doesn't feel any urgency to reach out and embrace a church across the street or city. The attitude is: "We're doing our thing, and they're doing theirs; God bless 'em." But let the lost begin to press into our meeting houses by the thousands, let the sick begin to be lowered through the ceilings, let the beggars and vagabonds abandon their "will work for food" signs and start to flood our sanctuaries and suddenly we'll be like those in Luke 5:7: "They signaled to their partners in the other boat to come and help them. And they came and filled their boats." When the net we have fashioned begins to break under the strain of harvest, we'll surely call out to one another for help at the cost of our own agendas! *God, give us harvest!* It's the only thing that will tear down the walls of religion once and for all.

The conferences we attend next year won't have the same format as they do this year. The time to just convene will be turned into a time to invade. We'll be busy at more doing than we are hearing. Teams will be mobilized and released into targeted areas of host cities. Reports will tell each night of the souls who were saved and the bodies healed. Prophetic conferences will become mass baptismals as hundreds receive Christ and water baptism. A weeklong conference will turn into months of training and equipping as the hundreds, even thousands, who got saved during that conference hunger and thirst for more. What started as a week will explode into revival and harvest as the lost fill auditoriums and church buildings until fields and parking lots become the norm for meetings and gatherings.

Get ready, saints! The face of Christianity is about to be transfigured! What we saw in the mirror of the "perfect law of liberty" yesterday isn't what we're going to see tomorrow! The old, dry bones of the wilderness experience will have to lie there. We're crossing over into the Promised Land! We're about to possess the land the Lord has allotted us! The words of Joshua will ring through the camp of God once again: "Sanctify yourselves, for tomorrow the Lord will do wonders among you" (Josh. 3:5).

The Church can't survive any longer on the old manna, the old experience. As they did in Joshua 5, we must begin to eat the fruit of Canaan and partake of the Lord's promises of revival and harvest. "Then the manna ceased on the day after they had eaten the produce of the land; and the children of Israel no longer had manna, but they ate the food of the land of Canaan that year" (Josh. 5:12). We must begin to hunger for and desire a greater manifestation of His grace and power to affect our city and streets. A pat prayer won't suffice in this new millennium. God is looking for "*doers of the word, not hearers only*" (see James 1:22). He wants warriors who will cross the Jordan of tradition and begin to radically possess the land, leaders who will mobilize the troops and train them for battle and confrontation, and pastors who will dare to become partners with churches of other denominations and races for the gospel's sake. He's looking for people who aren't ashamed of the gospel of Jesus Christ.

This is the sound that will carry us into the deep, "Launch out into the deep and let down your nets for a catch" (see Luke 5:4). This is the courage that will sustain the coming move of God. This is the heart attitude that will compel a generation of youths to "offer up their bodies as a living sacrifice" (see Rom. 12:1) instead of on the altars of drugs and sex. Nothing less will move them. Nothing less will affect them. God, give us a "council of war" so we may "please Him who enlisted [us] as [soldiers]" (2 Tim. 2:4)!

CHAPTER 21

HELL IS FOR REAL

Jesus tells a story in Luke 16 of the rich man and the poor man. The rich man cried out, "Father Abraham, have mercy on me, and send Lazarus that he may dip the tip of his finger in water and cool my tongue for I am tormented in the flame" (Luke 16:24). It is clear what this man was going through. This is one of the rare times that Jesus does not refer to this as a parable or an example. He was speaking of it as a reality.

Abraham's response is even more revealing, "Son, remember that in your lifetime you received your good things, and likewise Lazarus evil things; but now he is comforted and you are tormented" (Luke 16:25). The word *odunao* (od-oo-nah'-o) literally means "sorrow or torment." Hell is a reality, and that is why Christ was crucified. "But we preach Christ crucified, unto the Jews a stumbling block, and unto the Greeks foolishness" (1 Cor. 1:23). It may seem foolish or beyond reason that Christ had to die for us. But it is still as relevant now as it was centuries ago. No wonder then that Paul was so determined, "For I determined not to know any thing among you, save Jesus

Christ, and Him crucified" (1 Cor. 2:2). Let us all have that same determination.

What is also startling is that there is a place where the mercy of God does not reach. The rich man's plea of "Father Abraham, have mercy on me" did not work in this place of torment. No wonder the prophet Isaiah told us, "Seek ye the Lord while He may be found, call ye upon Him while He is near" (Isa. 55:6, KJV). God's mercy is now. We must take full advantage of this mercy and demonstrate it everywhere we go. Today is the day of salvation; tomorrow may be the day of judgment. "For we must all appear before the judgment seat of Christ; that every one may receive the things done in his body, according to that he hath done, whether it be good or bad" (2 Cor. 5:10, KJV).

Hell is the motivating factor for evangelism! Knowing this, Paul exclaimed, "For though I preach the gospel, I have nothing to glory of: for necessity is laid upon me; yea, woe is unto me, if I preach not the gospel" (1 Cor. 9:16, KJV). God give us all that necessity! Paul must have had the same revelation as Jesus did in Luke chapter 16 when he said, "Knowing therefore the terror of the Lord, we persuade men..." (2 Cor. 5:11, KJV). There is an awful terror awaiting those who reject the blood of Jesus, but there is also awesome mercy for those who do not. Remember Jesus' mercy to the thief on the cross? "And he said unto Jesus, Lord, remember me when Thou comest into Thy kingdom. And Jesus said unto him, Verily I say unto thee, Today shalt thou be with Me in paradise" (Luke 23:42-43, KJV). Whether it is a thief or murderer on death row, a druggie or a prostitute, a rich man or a poor man, one whisper of His name can set them free. "O wretched man that I am! Who shall deliver me from the body of this death? I thank God through Jesus Christ our Lord" (Rom. 7:24-25, KJV).

It is shocking to imagine that everyone who has ignored Christ in this life is crying out from their own torment and begging us to go and preach the gospel. If the Lord's commands are not enough, maybe the cries of hell will be: "Then he said, I pray thee therefore, father, that thou wouldest send him to my father's house: For I have five brethren; that he may testify unto them, lest they also come into this place of torment" (Luke 16:27-28, KJV).

A MEDITATION ON LAMENTATIONS 2:19

Still their blood cries out to Me,
From the top of every street,
The little ones who have no place to go,
The runaway, who's convinced he has no home.

This impure religion is a smoke in My eyes,
The ones I love and died for you've hated and despised.
They walk and wander on the city streets,
Broken and distressed, begging for something to eat.

Will you love the least of these?
Will you bring them unto Me?
Or will you continue to be deaf to their cries;
Will you ignore and let My children die?

Arise! Cry out in the night!
Give no rest to your eyes!
Until every one of them has a place to lay their head,
Until every hungry belly is fed.
How dare you hold back the oil and the wine!

I will require every drop that you have wasted,
Ignoring their pain, turning your eyes from their angry faces,
Angry at the way you have represented My name,
Building your kingdoms, seeking fortune and fame,
I am ashamed to call you by My name.

This is a people that I will seek,
Ones who have forsaken this life and set their affections on Me,

Who will be a drink offering for the least of these,
Knowing that they have really done it unto Me.

Pour out your heart like water before the face of the Lord!
Bind up the wounds of the rejected and torn;
Pour in the oil and wine to heal their wounds,
The downcast and abused,
The orphans and the bruised.

Who will bring them into their house?
Who will not just take in, but pour out?
"Who among you," says the Lord?

So they pine away, in boxes and alleyways,
No one to love them and show them the Way.
Millions die on your city streets,
Yet you cry out, "More Lord, More for me!"

Rachel is weeping because her children are no more;
They've cried out, but you've ignored.
Now is the time to open your eyes,
To finally realize, it was for these that I died,
That I gave My life,
It is time…

Time to give all that you have for the gospel's sake;
Let this world know the power of My name;
Deliver them from their sorrow and shame;
Relieve them of their anger and pain.

Now hear Me, My people,
Go to the hungry ones, the ones who have no home,
The ones who are broken, lost, and alone,
Tell them there is a Savior who is acquainted with all their ways;
They are not forgotten, I know them by name!

Even in the womb I called them by name!
Tell them I died that they could have life,
That I already paid the price, that they would not have to die!

Hurry! Go out into the highways and the byways
And compel them to come in!

Tell them that I will love them and will forgive them of
their sin!
That I truly am their friend!

Now hear Me, My shepherds,
It is time to unlock the doors and let them inside,
To provide a shelter from the storm,
A place to hide.

To feed and to clothe,
And let the little children know,
That there is hope, yes, there is Hope.
It is time…

If you do not hasten to My word,
I will remove your candlestick from its place,
And you will bear your own shame,
Because you have refused to obey.

Thrust out!
Thrust out!
Laborers move out!
It is your hour;
Signs and wonders will follow you as you obey!

Hastening the coming day
Of the Lord.
Psalm 2:8 shall be fulfilled in this hour,
As I declare to the nations My power.

CHAPTER 22

HELL'S
BEST-KEPT SECRET

"Brother Saul, the Lord Jesus, who appeared to you on the road as you came, has sent me that you may receive your sight and be filled with the Holy Spirit." Immediately there fell from his eyes something like scales, and he received his sight at once (Acts 9:17-18).

Until the scales fell off of Saul's eyes, though he had experienced salvation and a dramatic conversion, he had no revelation of his destiny and imminent impact on the world. He was blind. Paul was hell's best-kept secret. So long as the scales of human frailty and unbelief clung to him, he was helpless. Saul was no great orator as he hid at the house of one called Judas. No rumors of apostle were heard that day, only fear and superstition as Saul clung to life blindly and ignorantly. He was ignorant of the magnitude of the divine call suspended over him in the Spirit.

The world is filled with "Sauls" who haven't comprehended the depth of the call. They walk through life with scales of normality and unbelief, convinced that God could never really use them. Faithless in their heart, disabling their faith, they walk through life captured by the enemy's scheme. The enemy is always plotting to discourage and question the divine election buried in the soil of their hearts that's waiting, growing, and ever ready to explode! Until Saul was confronted with revelation, he was in constant conflict with God's purposes. He "kicked against the pricks" (Acts 9:5, KJV). But once the revelation of Jesus shook him from the firm foundation of religion where he stood, he was awestruck. He was "transformed into the image of Jesus Christ" (see 2 Cor. 3:18). He went "from glory to glory" in a twinkling of an eye.

Apostasy became an apostle, and the synagogue reeled from the aftershock of this revelation. Hell's best-kept secret was revealed, and nothing could quench the fire of revelation in Paul's heart. He blazed with confirmation of God's perfect will. He pioneered in a world of unbelief. He made giant leaps of faith that millions followed to their destiny. Paul understood who he was: "Paul, called to be an apostle of Jesus Christ through the will of God" (1 Cor. 1:1). Paul had a revelation of Jesus Christ. Until there's revelation, there's no illumination. The scales are all we see. No light, no hope, no call. Just darkness. We are blind—blind to the infinite purpose of God in our lives.

We live from book to book, conference to conference, always hoping something extraordinary will happen to us and that some great revelation will arrest us and we'll be changed. But we're not willing to be shaken and removed from our foundation of truth as we understand it. We race from one conference to the next, never willing to just simply sit at His feet and be able to boldly say with Paul, "But I make known to you, brethren, that the gospel which was preached by me is not according to man. For I neither received it from man, nor was I taught it, *but it came through the revelation of Jesus Christ*" (Gal. 1:11-12).

The revelation of Jesus Christ! This was Paul's secret! His nights in the deep, his years in the desert, and his time with Jesus were what made him great—what made him an apostle and general of God. John didn't make him an apostle; Peter didn't pass the apostolic mantle on to him. It was only a revelation of who Jesus was that gave him his medals. Paul boasted of these medals later in his life: "From now on let no one bother me, for I bear in my body the marks of the Lord Jesus" (Gal. 6:17).

Paul carried His scars. They were the proof of the long nights alone when "all men forsook me" (2 Tim. 4:16, KJV). Paul knew the secret of isolation—not separation from the Body—but the isolation that led to revelation that then inevitably led to transformation. Jesus knew the secret of this in His own life: "Rising up a great while before day, He went out, and departed into a solitary place, and there prayed" (Mark 1:35, KJV). In this hour the treasures out of darkness will be awarded to those who enter their closet and close the door. They will be awarded to those who know the impact of the secret place. There they'll receive a crown.

Hell's best-kept secret is you—every one of you who reads this and every one of you who hungers and thirsts for righteousness with an insatiable appetite for Jesus. More than conferences and public addresses, you need Him! You need to see His face! You need to, like Moses, see His glory! Only that will fill the deep void in your spirit that longs to be filled. And from that place you will emerge like Paul emerged in Acts 9:20, which says, "immediately he preached the Christ in the synagogues, that He is the Son of God." Hell will reel from the impact of your revelation of who you are in Christ. You are "created in Christ Jesus for good works, which God prepared beforehand that we should walk in them" (Eph. 2:10). You will enter the world as

Paul did and bring a revelation of Jesus Christ. You will move mountains of religion and shake nations. You are hell's best-kept secret.

CHAPTER 23

HABAKKUK'S PRAYER

O Lord I have heard Your speech and was afraid; O Lord, revive Your work in the midst of the years! In the midst of the years make it known; **in wrath remember mercy** (Habakkuk 3:2).

The name *Habakkuk* means "embrace." Habakkuk did not stand afar off at the fringes of Israel and prophesy destruction like a spectator waiting for the gun to go off. No! He embraced Israel, pleaded for her repentance, and petitioned for the Lord's mercy to triumph over His judgment. God took Habakkuk from a place of imminent defeat, "O Lord, how long shall I cry, and You will not hear" (Hab. 1:2a) to a place of faith and victory, "The Lord God is my strength; He will make my feet like deer's feet, and He will make me walk on my high hills" (Hab. 3:19).

Even in the midst of certain invasion and captivity Habakkuk glimpsed beyond the temporal into the eternal and saw God's mercy and faithfulness. In his fear and flesh he finally comprehended, "But the just shall live by his faith" (Hab. 2:4b).

Today, in the midst of national turmoil and governmental intrigue, a prophetic chorus will rise from the din of defeat to herald a greater Power, a greater Glory, and a greater God who is not bound by elemental and human limitations. "He who is in [me] is greater than he who is in the world" (1 John 4:4).

Habakkuk saw a greater glory than that present in Israel. He saw something on the horizon that eclipsed the present distress and destruction. Once he saw it he exclaimed, "For the earth will be filled with the knowledge of the glory of the Lord, as the waters cover the sea" (Hab. 2:14). From sackcloth and ashes arose a vision of a greater day and a greater time when the Lord of Hosts would visit His people and restore His glory to them. If we are to prophesy with any eternal effect, we too must see beyond the veil of fears and current affairs and see Him high and lifted up! We must see Him transfigured and like lightning! Only from that place of revelation will we ever have the understanding to pray with Habakkuk, "In wrath remember mercy" (Hab. 3:2).

Fear no longer gripped Habakkuk's heart. Fear no longer influenced his ministry and words. He had come to the divine conclusion, "Though the fig tree may not blossom, nor fruit be on the vines; though the labor of the olive may fail, and the fields yield no food...Yet I will rejoice in the Lord, I will joy in the God of my salvation" (Hab. 3:17-18). In his temptation he saw His salvation! In derision and confusion he glimpsed God's salvation! He wasn't ruled by fear, but by faith! A person who prophesies from fear and intimidation breeds only the same. One must glimpse the high places, walk with hind's feet, and breathe the rarefied air of Heaven. Only then will he or she bring His glory in their wake and declare with Habakkuk, "His glory covered the heavens, and the earth was full of His praise" (Hab. 3:3b).

Modern-day prophecy must come to this place of inspiration—the place where their words and declarations are influenced by faith, not fear. Their faith must be in a God who transcends all current predictions and prognostications. A God "who loves the world so much that He gave His only begotten Son. That whoever would just believe in Him would *not* perish but have everlasting life" (John 3:16). When our hearts are ruled by that kind of love and when our ministries are ablaze with that kind of passion, then our words and decrees will not bring hopelessness, but rather like Paul, we will "rejoice in hope of the glory of God" (Rom. 5:2). We see and hope for a greater glory coming! We expect and anticipate a greater and more glorious hour to visit us! We grasp as did all the prophets, " 'The glory of this latter temple shall be greater than the former,' says the Lord of Hosts" (Hag. 2:9a).

The glory of God will be our hope and our anchor, our mainstay and our Rock, "that we should no longer be children, tossed to and fro and carried about with every wind of doctrine...but, speaking the truth in love, may grow up in all things into Him who is the head—Christ" (Eph. 4:14-15). We will walk the earth in knowledge of that glory "as the waters cover the sea." We won't be influenced by "wars and rumors of wars." But we will comprehend what it meant when Jesus prayed, "And the glory which You gave Me I have given them, that they may be one just as We are one." We will be like Him. "Being transformed into the same image from glory to glory" (2 Cor. 3:18).

Only then will the masses of pierced and tattooed bodies heed our words. Only then will the derelict and heretic come to His feet to be washed. Then, and only then, will the unloved and unlovely open their hearts and minds and be saved. As long as we parade our own personalized doctrines and treatises they will perish as we prophesy. We must get hold of His heart, His glory, and His willingness to redeem even the most decadent! God is not standing over the nations of the world with a hammer of judgment, but rather with a hand that is pierced and bleeding, aching for His people to grasp this kind of Love, and pour out to the earth like He did as they lifted Him up. The promise still remains true: "And I, if I am lifted up from the earth, will draw all peoples to Myself" (John 12:32).

CHAPTER 24

LIONS OF REVIVAL

The wicked flee when no man pursues, but the righteous are bold as lions (Proverbs 28:1, KJV).

In an hour of political unrest and international upheaval, God is calling for lions—lions bold in their obedience, radical in their devotion, and spiritually prepared for battle. Jesus was born for war. First John 3:8 states in no uncertain terms: "For this *purpose* the Son of God was manifested, that He might destroy the works of the devil." Jesus came to usurp the strongholds of the devil and establish righteousness in the hearts of men. Spiritual warfare is to see the hearts of battered, bruised humanity bound up in His love.

Spiritual warfare isn't limited to long hours of prayer or longer days of fasting; it involves piercing the darkness that holds the masses captive and invading the boundaries of hell, crying, "*Give them back!*" Spiritual warfare consists of setting the captives free, binding up the brokenhearted, and opening the prison to them who are bound, leaving footprints leading to the

Mount of Transfiguration and affecting a city, a generation, and a nation. This is war (see Luke 4:17-18).

This act of, or the ability to, war is delivered to the spirit of every born-again believer. He has transferred the keys of the Kingdom to His Church "to the intent that now unto the principalities and powers in heavenly places might be known *by the church* the manifold wisdom of God" (Eph. 3:10, KJV). He has given this charge to each of His servants: "Occupy till I come" (Luke 19:13, KJV). The word *occupy* is a military term; it's aggressive and it's violent. It means to take territory and not only overcome the resistance, but to *occupy and keep it!*

This is war! We are His warriors. YOU are His warrior. In you, revival is wrapped up and waiting to be exposed. In you, an effectual power waits to explode. It's time for the substance of revival that lies dormant in most of us to be loosed and ignited. Revival is only a step, a breath away. It's waiting inside of you like a volcano—turbulent, tumultuous, and fervent. It will only be released as you step from the safe confines of religion and thrust out into the deep of your city streets, speaking to the tomb of despair: "Lazarus, come forth!"

God is forming the heart of the Lion of Judah in the hearts of His people so that we will pursue rather than *be* pursued. We will be aggressive instead of being passive. We will be "terrible as an army with banners" (Song of Sol. 6:4b, KJV). We will be the lion, the hunter, not the hunted. In the early Church they prayed the prayer of the lion: "And now, Lord, behold their threatenings: and grant to Thy servants, that with all *boldness* they may speak Thy word" (Acts 4:29, KJV). We dare not do any less.

Boldness, Lord! Give us boldness to do Your will no matter what the cost! To follow You no matter the loss! To go into all the world to save that which is lost! Lord, give us boldness!

Is that your prayer? From this day forth, make it what you breathe. Boldness. Lord, give me boldness. Paul could do nothing less in the face of the wild beasts of Ephesus, the danger of high-waymen, the hurtling stones of the religious, and the chanting mobs of pagans! He prayed, "And for me, that utterance may be given unto me, that I may open my mouth *boldly*, to make known the mystery of the gospel" (Eph. 6:19, KJV). We can do no less. We can do no less!

God forbid that our streets remain silent to the witness of Christ. God forbid that the gangs and drug pushers occupy our neighborhoods instead of vigilant Christians. God forbid that we remain on this road of apathy and indifference as children in every city are ravaged and wrecked by sin. God forbid that church remains just a place to drink espresso and read a good book. God forbid that the prayer meeting stands dormant and cold in the average church, believers more content to play than pray. God forbid that we do not begin to train our people to evangelize and be a personal impact in every public place, releasing revival wherever they walk. God forbid that we as leaders aren't more concerned with the state of our streets and school buildings than we are of our building projects and church-growth programs.

I'll tell you the key to church growth! *Revival!* Create a church of revivalists who spark flames of revival and power wherever the soles of their feet tread! We must begin to teach every man, woman, and child that revival, the substance of it, is in them. They are "living epistles," spreading the passion of Christ in every place they go and every building they step into. They are the embodiment of revival.

Why are you here? To what purpose were you born? Do you have a reason for existing? Listen to the words of Christ to His servant Paul:

> For I have appeared to you for this **purpose**, to make you a minister and a witness both of the things which you have seen and of the things which I will yet reveal to you...to open their eyes, in order to turn them from darkness to light, and from the

power of Satan to God, that they may receive forgiveness of sins and inheritance among those who are sanctified by faith in Me (Acts 26:16-18).

The very purpose that we were created for is to hold Him in human hearts and unleash His power and grace to a dying and crippled world. This is the purpose God has given to each one of us who claims Him as Lord. We are soldiers on a mission of salvation to set the captives free. "Because as He is, so are we in this world" (1 John 4:17).

You have a purpose! You have an eternal destiny to be His voice! His heart! His hands! His feet! Your purpose is to profoundly affect the world around you. You are an ambassador of Christ, a minister of reconciliation, and a peacemaker. You are called to bring peace to the storm of life that rages in the heart of the lost. You are the one He's called to pour out oil and wine into the wounds of the beaten and wasted welfare recipient. You are the one! To you has He commanded: "Go ye into all the world and preach the gospel" (Mark 16:15, KJV).

You have a purpose! You have a reason for living and breathing, for in Him you move and have your being; in Him you thrust out into the darkness and cry, "Let there be light!" He has entrusted such responsibility to you! Our claim must be Paul's: "Woe is unto me if I preach not the gospel" (1 Cor. 9:16, KJV). We are the ones who must carry the blazing torch of His love into the uttermost parts of the earth. We are the ones who must make disciples of all men, baptizing them in the name of the Father, the Son, and the Holy Spirit. We are the ones who must break the walls of bondage that manipulate and molest the children who wander to and fro in the city streets. I am the one. You are the one.

"How?" you ask. "How can I accomplish such a thing?" "Who am I to presume such feats?" "What could I possibly do in such a dark world?" First, you must understand that it's not *you* who does it! It's the Spirit of your Father who is *in* you that will demonstrate such deeds! It's the *Lion* who lives inside of you! He's the One who will supernaturally express His power in you to the world! "I am crucified with Christ: nevertheless I live; yet not I, Christ liveth in me" (Gal. 2:20a, KJV)! Christ longs to manifest Himself in the power of revival. He's waiting only for you to cry out, "Here am I, send me!" Peter replied to the Lord in his day, "Lo, we have left all and followed you!" Paul confessed, "For me to live is Christ, and to die is gain" (Phil. 1:21, KJV). He's waiting only for us "to present our bodies as a living sacrifice" (see Rom. 12:1) and to live the same kind of life.

He's the One who makes fruit pickers into prophets (see Amos 7:14)! He made a shepherd boy a king (see 1 Sam. 16:11-13); fishermen into apostles (see Matt. 4:19); and prostitutes into princesses (see John 8:11). He's the One who's calling you to be His voice "crying in the wilderness, make straight paths for the Lord" (see Mark 1:3).

"Now when they saw the *boldness* of Peter and John, and perceived that they were unlearned and ignorant men, they marveled; and they took knowledge of them, that they had been with Jesus" (Acts 4:13, KJV). That's the foremost qualification of revival—have you been with the Master?

Fear is the fatal enemy of the soldier of the cross. Through fear the enemy can disable what once was powerful and lethal in the Father's hands. Through fear the devil can shut up the saints in the upper room, ever waiting and never doing. It's his most formidable weapon against the Church. It paralyzes and cripples the limbs of the Body, causing them to be stunted and twisted.

The only antidote for this disease is the all-consuming love of Jesus Christ. His love will drive out the dark tendrils of fear from the believer's heart, making a coward into a warrior. Peter was a coward on the day of Christ's arrest. A few weeks later he was a powerful preacher to rioting Israel! Only the love of Jesus could do such a thing! Only the explosive love of Jesus can transform a passive Church into an aggressive army that will not only co-exist with the world, but also possess it, and not only pray against the psychics and pimps, but also boldly step into their domain and declare His ownership and His dominion. This is the command from our heavenly headquarters: "As the Father has sent Me, so send I you!" (see John 20:21). Fear still torments; His love still casts it out. We must again be, "Men that have hazarded their lives for the name of our Lord Jesus Christ" (Acts 15:26, KJV).

"AWAY IN A MANGER"

Away in a manger was the child born,
no silver and gold with its tapestries adorned,
but among shepherds and kings did this baby cry,
with thieves and prostitutes did this same child die...

He walked among the simple, speaking parables to the wise,
healing all who were sick, opening the blind man's eyes.
No one could explain from where He had come;
no one could explain the things that He had done...

The wise man sat perplexed as the children ran into His hands,
the simple and the sick could understand,
this was the Father's perfect plan!
The Messiah, the King, the Lamb!

Now around the manger a cathedral men build,
pushing away the children, disregarding the Father's will,
they adorn it with gold and silver and everything nice,
but the priceless ones He died for they despise...

They build it as if to reach the sky,
thinking that quantity will suffice,
to feed the ones begging in the streets,
while all along Jesus says, "Bring them unto Me..."

Away in a manger a child was born,
no silver and gold with its tapestries adorned,
but among shepherds and kings did this baby cry,
with thieves and prostitutes did this same child die...

CHAPTER 25

WHO WILL
STAND IN THE GAP?

When Jesus was on this earth in physical form, He became a mediator between God and man. What made Him such an effective negotiator between Heaven and earth? Besides the obvious, His deity and nobility, what really created such a revolution between social and religious hostilities? The answer is simple: He was with the people. He ate with them, He sat and socialized with them, and in many cultural interpretations, He was one of them. In Jesus' meteoric and nearly overnight success as He ascended from "son of Joseph and Mary" to the Son of God, He never forgot the people. He never allowed His religious standing to regulate His social involvement and influence. In other words, He met the people where they were. Whether this was at the wedding of Cana, in the tax collector's home, or in the literal immersing of Himself in the massive crowds that followed Him, Jesus the prophet, Jesus the apostle, and Jesus God never distanced Himself from the social and relevant needs of the people around Him.

Today we see an opposite regression from the social and religious revolution Jesus initiated. Now, as ministers and leaders progress up the ministry ladder of popularity, they distance themselves from the common man at the same time. What it finally becomes is a segregated group or body that meets in conferences and meetings with very limited genres of social representation. Modern-day prophets fail to express the real need of the cities and people around them because *they are no longer a part of the people and the cities around them!* They have limited themselves to the immediate influence of those drawn to their ministries. Ask the visiting prophet when he last went to a tavern in his city to sit and hear the heart of the people? Or went to a mall and hung out with the youth to hear firsthand their needs and concerns? Or walked in America's ghettos to see the tragic plight of millions of people? Nine out of ten times they have not. They have fallen prey to the modern methodology of ministry that caters to the minority—the saved—rather than the majority—the lost.

What kind of strain and pressure does this apply to the heart and possible salvation of those in these cities and regions? The answer is complex. What we have created in modern ministry is the opposite of what Christ set in motion in His. He promoted and catered to the sinner. We distance ourselves and, even worse, create environments in our conferences and churches that alienate and push away the lost or unsaved. The modern-day prophet has become a celebrity instead of an advocate and friend of the people. We have reversed the very cycle of social and religious reformation that Jesus initiated 2,000 years ago in Jerusalem. He was faced with many, if not more, of the social strains we are faced with today, i.e. Jews and Gentiles (different races), Pharisees and Sadducees (different denominations), and the ancient struggle of gender and where it fits into our religious experience. Jesus confronted these issues head-on and prevented the disease of social and religious prejudice that modern ministries have allowed today. We must re-evaluate everything we do. We need an infusion of His heart into our ministries. We must not allow another moment to pass without using the platforms of our conferences and personalities as stages set for outreach and revival. We must cast our net on the other side of modern methods and ministry.

Just through our concept of conferences we are feeding this disease. If we do not begin to introduce the Church to the lost and struggling world around us, how can we ever entertain the idea of social transformation? We teach the opposite in our religious dress codes and our demeanor and attitudes. We shout at a world that is spiritually unaware, "Unless you somehow attain our spiritual prowess you can never be saved, and your level of social standing is not good enough to qualify you into our elite groups of religious expression." It is shocking that modern leaders still find it necessary to even wear a tie. This small act of religious protocol can strengthen and lengthen the gap between religious idealism and true revival. How long will we permit this before we take on the unadulterated nature of Jesus and baptize ourselves into humanity? Most of what we do today would be unacceptable in Jesus' group of disciples. Rather, it would fit fairly well in the temples of the Pharisees and Sadducees. We must reverse this cycle of separation and spiritual segregation now if we are ever going to experience the magnitude of harvest prophesied and intended for this present generation. We have to step up to the spiritual Jordan of our time and say to John, "Suffer it to be so now" (Matt. 3:15, KJV), thus condescending and putting ourselves at the same level of those we are ministering to.

The answer is simple—JESUS. But the process to undo centuries of religious jargon and dispensation is not. We are faced with a problem of epic proportions. There is a road less traveled that, if taken, can exponentially change the religious landscape around us. We have to realize that any personality or notoriety that is given to us is ultimately for harvest. Jesus was no stranger to notoriety or fame: "And Jesus returned in the power of the Spirit into Galilee: and there went out a fame of Him through all the region round about" (Luke 4:14, KJV). But we see a balance at work here that most evangelists and ministers forget, "And Jesus saith unto him, See thou tell no man; but go thy way, shew thyself to the priest, and offer the gift that Moses commanded, for a testimony unto them" (Matt. 8:4, KJV). This was after the notable miracle done for the man with leprosy. There is a time for promotion, but there is also a time to be quiet. We have put the knife to the throat of influence in modern culture because of our inability to relate to the common man and woman in our lifestyles. Jesus did just the opposite. He ate with them, sat with them, and really was a part of their entire living experience. He avoided any undue social pressure to perform. To a large degree, we have become performers in our ministries because of this social pressure applied from the conferences and crowds around us. We have given them a show and now they expect a show every time; thus the people outside this experience perish.

The Old Testament model of the temple holds a secret to modern revival and outreach. Let's look at this more carefully. The outer court was where most of the transactions between the social and religious classes occurred. The inner court evolved into a more intimate experience between God and the priest, which was ultimately for the people. Finally, there was the Holy of Holies. This was a place where only the High Priest could tend to the altar for the sins of all the people as well as himself once a year. How can this apply today? Today, our Holy of Holies is obvious. When we are saved and washed in the blood of Christ, we enter this place freely. The inner court is the place of healing and introduction to this intimacy and reality. The outer court is the missing link today in church and ministry—*a place that the common man can come freely to taste and see that the Lord is good.*

In the Old Testament model of the temple, if someone unclean came into the Holy of Holies (or anyone other than the priest for that matter), they died! How many "deaths" of modern revivals have occurred because we have tried to force a generation into the Holy of Holies instead of first bringing them into an outer-court place of meeting or experience? We need to institute outer courts into our conferences and our churches— a place where the world can come and feel normal. This may come as a shock to many, but the world does not wear a tie.

"And the Word was made flesh, and dwelt among us, (and we beheld His glory)" (John 1:14a, KJV). Jesus came to earth and *dwelt among us.* He did not separate Himself from the world, but rather, He came into it with forceful love and compassion. The idea that Jesus dwelt among us should be the model that our ministries follow—we must also dwell among them! Jesus has become "in the flesh" again every time we take Him to the modern-day marketplaces of the world. He becomes "in the flesh" every time we touch someone in need or we love one another as He has loved us. The only way to transcend contemporary religious dogma, which has blurred who He really is, is to become Him in the flesh again and personally interact with the world around us. We need to join their clubs, go to their meetings, attend their social gatherings and invade every venue of society with His power and glory. That is the only way to fulfill the second sentence in John 1:14: "and we beheld His glory" (KJV).

How will they ever behold His glory when it is fish-bowled in conferences and private Christian experiences, confined to church groups and settings? We must create an "outer court" experience to then marry our conferences with their present reality of existence. We must do it now or become another dispensation or spot on church history books, rather than the monumental prophetic generation of impact and influence previously prophesied.

"For we do not have a High Priest who cannot sympathize with our weaknesses, but who was in all points tempted as we are—yet without sin" (Heb. 4:15). This speaks of a Jesus who associated Himself with the people on every social and religious level. He identified with His generation to ultimately reach His generation. He was separate and at the same time not unequally yoked. Modern doctrine has created an entire exposé on the idea of being "unequally yoked" and its relationship between Christians and the world. We have determined "unequally yoked" to mean that we should not associate with the lost on their social levels. This is completely out of context and not in the paradigm of Christ's thinking or lifestyle. How did He justify then sitting with the drunkards and the gluttons? What we call a "party" today, Jesus called an opportunity. He justified His lifestyle in one eloquent and brilliant response to His critics, "I have not come to call the righteous, but sinners, to repentance" (Luke 5:32). This new breed of priests and prophets today will practice this same approach to the social world around them. They will have the inept understanding that they are in this world to be the light of the world, not a hidden object of religious affection.

"And as they that bare the ark were come unto Jordan, and the feet of the priests that bare the ark were dipped in the brim of the water, (for Jordan overflows all his banks all the time of harvest)" (Josh. 3:15, KJV). As the great army of Israel was crossing the Jordan into Canaan, notice who led the way in this campaign: the priests. They were not watching on closed-circuit TV or in isolated offices. They were the first ones to embark on this epic journey to blaze a trail for those that followed.

Notice also the season in which the priests were called to lead this march. It was the season of harvest, when the banks of the Jordan were overflowing. In this modern moment of unparalleled harvest, we as leaders and priests are being called on again to lead the company of Christians into battle. What awaited them across the river was not just milk and honey, it was epic battle. They had giants to slay and cities to possess. The same landscape of possession awaits us. Can we delay any longer? Can we dare stand behind the pulpit and be rushed out the door as the final note is played any longer? Can we continue to allow the catering and socializing that promote us to pedestals rather than divine power?

The social structure of our meetings only widens the margin between the world and the Church. Our special seating and vying for position and the star treatment afforded to those who speak cause the lost to shrink in the back row with the pervading feeling that they can never measure up to such an elite, god-like group. This is appalling to a Jesus who allowed dirty children to interrupt His message, sick homeless men to take precedence over His entourage, and prostitutes to approach Him as He met with religious dignitaries. This is the Jesus the world is still desperately seeking. Are they seeing Him in us?

CHAPTER 26

KEEPERS OF THE
FLAME OF REVIVAL

Throughout the Old Testament, the role of the priest is demonstrated. It seems that above all, he was the keeper of the inner flame, the temple "maintenance man," always preparing, positioning, and possessing the holy things. He was a mediator, a teacher, and, at times, a prophet. As the era of Old and New Testament merged, a transition took place. The role of the priest evolved to an even higher and more important role as the priest became intercessor, teacher, and evangelist.

An evolution takes place from Levitical priesthood, which consists of being more or less a servant of the temple duties, repetitiously divvying out the daily ritual of priesthood, to a greater light and a greater fire: Melchizedek. *Melchizedek* literally means: "fire (literally or figuratively, specifically, lightning): fiery, fire." The old, cold methodical position had been swallowed up by the fiery office of the New Testament priest or revivalist. It is no wonder then that on the Mount of Transfiguration,

Jesus' countenance was "like lightning, and His raiment white as snow" (Matt. 28: 3, KJV). He was "a priest forever according to the order of Melchizedek" (Heb. 7:17). His steps we now follow. Jesus made this very clear when He said to us, "You are the light of the world" (Matt. 5:14).

This role of priest or priesthood is now coming to fruition. The New Testament priests were fire-starters, keepers of the holy flame of revival, and prophets in the house of God. A priest was not just a monotonous, mundane minister, but a fiery brand thrown into the cold harsh world to light her, a tender and keeper of the awesome flame of revival and spiritual renaissance that was dawning as the old gave way to the new. Modern-day priests are revivalists and evangelists. They are concerned about atmospheres and positioning, functions and offices that the Body can perform to sustain a spiritual awakening. They see people, not rituals and salvations, not numbers; they are the modern-day Samuels who keep the flames of reformation lit, which Eli (the old) had extinguished.

I would also like to establish that the priest now is an intercessor. In modern-day thinking, the priest is pastor, a worker of charity or hospitality, and/or an agent of religion or ritual. But in the New Testament, Jesus is an intercessor: "Wherefore He is able also to save them to the uttermost that come unto God by Him, seeing He ever liveth to make intercession for them" (Heb. 7:25, KJV). "Because as He is, so are we in this world" (1 John 4:17b, KJV). We, as kings and priests, bear this same manner or task. We are intercessors, prophets, apostles, and evangelists.

The Great High Priest of our faith made His role in the earth perfectly clear: "For the Son of man is come to save that which was lost" (Matt. 18:11, KJV). And again, "Then said Jesus to them...as My Father hath sent Me, even so send I you" (John 20:21, KJV). The modern-day priest is not only keeper of the inner flame, but a fire-starter and salvationist. He is an intercessor, one who stands in the gap between the porch and the altar and cries out, "Spare Thy people, O Lord, and give not Thine heritage to reproach" (Joel 2:17, KJV).

Each one of us is to be a king and priest. Revelation 1:6 (KJV) says, "And hath made us kings and priests unto God and His Father; to Him be glory and dominion forever and ever. Amen." The key word here is "made." Jesus has made us into this; we have not become this on our own accord. We are naturally religious. We have a tendency to revert back to the old, the ritual, and the predictable. In the flesh, we are priests after the old order, the Levite, the seed of Aaron. Jesus makes us priests after the new, which is really even more ancient, Melchizedek, king and priest. Read carefully:

> For this [Melchizedek], *king of Salem, priest of the most high God, who met Abraham returning from the slaughter of the kings, and blessed him; to whom also Abraham gave a tenth part of all; first being by interpretation King of righteousness, and after that also King of Salem, which is, King of peace; without father, without mother, without descent, having neither beginning of days, nor end of life; but made like unto the Son of God; abideth a priest continually* (Hebrews 7:1-3, KJV).

Awesome.

The old kingship was done away with in Christ, as in the symbolism here, "slaughter of the kings." The old has been "slaughtered," or done away with, as in the old connotation of priesthood and kingship. He has redefined it and refashioned it after His own image. That is why we are being changed into His image from glory to glory. We are taking on the nature of king and priest, becoming intercessors and revivalists moment by moment.

We are becoming the ones who stand in the gap, the people who reach out and touch the lost and unsaved, the ones who delegate authority, the people who station and position the Church for revival. We are the keepers of the holy flame of reformation and change, ever increasing unto that perfect day. We are ambassadors and reconcilers, bridging the gap between Jerusalem and Samaria—the Church and the world. You are His priest, His Samuel, and His David. You are the one to whom He has given this high and intense task—to stoke, to rebuild, and to kindle the ancient flames of revival. Do it with all diligence and zeal, O priest and intercessor of the Most High God!

CHAPTER 27

DON'T STOP AT THE BURNING BUSH

Now Moses kept the flock of Jethro his father in law, the priest of Midian: and he led the flock to the backside of the desert, and came to the mountain of God, even to Horeb. And the angel of the Lord appeared unto him in a flame of fire out of the midst of a bush: and he looked, and, behold, the bush burned with fire, and the bush was not consumed. And Moses said, I will now turn aside, and see this great sight, why the bush is not burnt (Exodus 3:1-3, KJV).

On his journey to Mount Horeb, Moses was startled at the sight of a burning bush, which surprisingly was not consumed. He stopped in awe and turned aside to look at it. There he heard from God. In this era of eternity, droves are beginning their ascent up their mountain, and, like Moses, are stopping at the burning bush, transfixed by it. Even more are camping at the burning bush and forgetting that the whole mountain of the

Lord still lies ahead of them. There are peaks of revelation, water-falls of prophetic refreshing, pools of transformation, and finally, at the top of the mountain itself, the place of transfiguration.

Still, so many on their journey up the mountain of the Lord are stopping at the burning bush—the place of past experiences and previous revelation. They are satisfied to exist off another man's revelation and truth and are unwilling to seek out their own illumination, which is hidden higher up the mountain. They see the crowds of onlookers gathered at the burning bush and assume that this must be the place that the Lord is taking them. Rarely, a few break away, drawn by the knowledge of Christ that calls to them from higher ground. They hear the words of Paul, "I count all things but loss for the excellency of the knowledge of Christ Jesus my Lord" (Phil. 3:8, KJV). They pull away from the contemporary attractions and revelations to climb higher up the mountain of the Lord. They are driven by one purpose: to see Him.

Along the way there are many sights to see, many phenom-ena and manifestations of His presence, and many wonderful gifts that various people have on display. Again, many are camped at these various places of manifestation and phenome-na, unwilling to go on any further. They stop there and quickly forget that the road leads ever-upward to that great pinnacle of His presence. These manifestations were only meant to be land-marks along the path to the top of the mountain, to Him. Yet many stop at the manifestations and remain paralyzed by phe-nomena. They sit at these plateaus of revelation and are satis-fied, oblivious to the cry coming from higher up calling out to them, "After these things I looked, and behold, a door standing open in heaven. And the first voice which I heard was like a trumpet speaking with me, saying, 'Come up here, and I will show you things which must take place after this' " (Rev. 4:1).

Another strange sight on the way up the mountain is the piles of debris discarded along the path. Various items that people had taken with them, convinced in their hearts that they would need them in their ascent up the mountain, were discarded along the way. With each step up, these things, which once seemed so necessary, become only burdens and distractions that had to be left behind. The voice of Paul echoed down the mountain again, "Set your affection on things above, not on things on the earth" (Col. 3:2, KJV). As the ascent continued and as the path became much more steep and narrow, it was critical that everything that weighed them down was cast aside while they progressed ever-upward.

Thunder and lightning could be seen at the top. At the top of the mountain of the Lord the travelers received their reward—their heart's desire—to see Him. At the top of the mountain they received their wings and were allowed to fly back down the mountain to the great valley of decision below. From that point on, each one could fly to the top of the mountain and back down again. They were free from the things of this world as they waited upon Him and He strengthened them. They came from the mountain filled with revelation and glory for the burdened and broken far below. From the top of the mountain they could see all of the nations of the world. Each eagle was sent from the mountain to the uttermost parts of the earth, filled with His glory and power.

Harvest had come upon the whole earth and these eagles were the harvesters. Those who had suffered the loss of all things while climbing up the mountain of the Lord were the last great army that was trusted with the souls of all the nations of the world. They were the gatekeepers of His glory and grace. A chosen generation and royal priesthood, they were willing to praise Him and live for Him with all of their hearts. They were the ones willing to strive for the upward call in Christ Jesus and would not settle for burning bushes of previous revelations or dispensations. They had to see Him. The echo still rings in their ears, *"Don't stop at the burning bush; continue up the mountain!"*

CHAPTER 28

HEAVEN, HOLLYWOOD, AND HISTORY'S GREATEST REVIVAL

Throughout modern history, satan has done his best to steal from Heaven the most talented musicians and artists to exploit their talents and gifts for the kingdom of darkness. This can be seen clearly in icons such as the Beatles and Elvis Presley. Their hearts beat with a spiritual passion but were never captured for Christ. What was intended to impact the nations for God was made rather to temporarily inspire a generation to rebel against God and His passion for them. Prophets and evangelists were disillusioned in their gifts and calling to worship the creation rather than the Creator.

Tragically, most of the prolific talent today is still ensnared in the world and its trappings. The most endearing music, memorable lyrics, and historical concerts are written on the pages of secular music. If you turn on any rock station, you will hear the passion and anger of this generation captured in each song and rhythm, and a generation is entranced by its beat. If you turn on any Christian station the most you will usually hear is a shallow, hollow sound that entertains Christians, rather than seeking to save souls by provoking and challenging this generation to Christ. It is no mystery then why the youth, both Christian and non-Christian alike, listen to secular radio stations and watch MTV more than they listen to or watch any Christian stations. We are still trying to entertain each other instead of making a sound that causes the masses to cry out, "God is truly among you" (1 Cor. 14:25).

If we are to ever reach this generation, *we must first get the heart of Christ for this generation.* We must invade every worldly space with the message of God's great grace. We have to take on the attitude of Philip in Acts chapter 8 and get up from our comfortable, Christian easy chair to rock the world with the sound of Heaven. I believe Philip was one of the first "rock stars." The whole city "saw and heard the miracles which Philip did" and were saved (see Acts 8:6). Philip then turned their eyes to the only Rock, the Rock that was Christ. If we are ever to have any level of success in this world we must do the same. We have to cast off our religious garb, our "Sunday go to church clothes," and start relating to a dying world. If we do not, if we refuse to make any adjustment to our spiritual attire and sound, if we do not make any attempt to accommodate this generation in our Sunday morning services, if we make no honest effort to reach out to the youth still hanging out on the corners smoking their cigarettes and listening to Ozzy Osbourne, mark these words, the blood of millions will be on our hands.

The greatest threshold of revival is standing at our church doors with pierced faces and tattoos. They stare hungrily at our steeples and altars, longing to be welcomed, not made to change. They want to be accepted, not rejected. To date, the treasure of Heaven's greatest revival is hidden in the fallow ground of these young hearts. They are waiting for the plow of love to be brought to them with the mercy and grace of Christ. Then and only then will we reap the immense talents and gifts of this generation. It is a generation poised like no other generation to reap world harvest and prepare the way of the Lord.

I pray that God would give us all eyes to see past the dark tapestries of modern music, the glam of Hollywood, and see the pearls of great price hidden there—mighty prophets and evangelists yet to take the stage of revival and history, missionaries of music able to reach the souls of this generation like no one in church today ever possibly could. God will redeem their fame and fortune to impact millions of children who already hang on to their every word and song. We need to pray for them, not judge them, and reach out to them, not condemn them!

God, give us the great revelation that the enemy's best are really God's best in disguise, waiting to be awakened to their divine destiny in Christ. God give us the eyes of Barnabas to see past Saul's reputation and infamy into God's purposes and plan for him while the rest of the Church was terrified of him. Take away the fear we have of the world that we can begin to invade it with Your passion and grace, now.

Hollywood and the music industry are not a dark spot on American history; rather, they are a seed bed for revival and global harvest. They draw the vision and dreams of the youth like moths to a flame and give them a place to grow. They are doing exactly what the Church should be doing, but are not. So, youth gravitate to these venues instead. The modern-day Church needs to be the flame that draws the vision and dreams of the youth and gives them the place to thrive and express themselves. The Church needs to become the stage on which the members of this generation act out their destiny and purpose. The church should not be a boring, predictable place where individual expression is discouraged and quenched. The institution of modern church needs to be turned upside down again so it can begin to facilitate the revival that God so longs to pour out on her. It is a revival that will draw the lost like bees to honey, a revival that will capture the creativity of this generation and harness it to reach the world. God, turn us upside down!

The day is coming when Christian programs will rival the ratings of MTV. The hour is coming where church will be a haven for late-night teens, closing down rave parties and dance clubs. The hour is coming when the church will be the greatest stage of individual expression as each person fulfills his or her role and purpose to reach the nations. The day is coming when Christians will have the vision and creative imagination surpassing Stephen King and Stephen Spielberg, a creativity that invades the motion picture industry with the radical message of Jesus Christ. The day is coming when the church will be transformed into a 24-hour outreach and safe harbor for the shipwrecked of mankind, the doors opened and hearts ready to receive them. The candle will never go out again in God's temple.

Chapter 29

A Prayer of Jesus

"Father, forgive My Church for leaving her first love. Forgive them for disregarding the reason that I had first come to this earth, to save that which was lost. Forgive them, Father, for overlooking the hurt and pain that stare at them every day from the streets and corners—the least of their brethren. Father, forgive them for the apathy and indifference that have blinded them from the greatest blessing: to give. Forgive them for knowing Me for so long and still not changing the world they live in. Father, forgive them.

"Father, forgive My shepherds and pastors for teaching a gospel of wealth instead of compassion and of gain rather than giving. Forgive them, Father, for leading My people astray with empty promises instead of demonstrating Your power. Forgive them for ignoring the widow and the orphan and yet, in false pretense, constructing bigger and grander buildings while Your children still wander to and fro in the streets. How quickly they have forgotten Your words, 'Howbeit the most High dwelleth not in temples made with hands; as saith the prophet, Heaven is

My throne, and earth is My footstool: what house will ye build Me? saith the Lord: or what is the place of My rest? Hath not My hand made all these things?' (Acts 7:48-50, KJV).

"Father, forgive them for disregarding our great commandment to 'Go into all the world and preach the gospel to every creature' (Mark 16:15). Father, have mercy on a Church that is so wealthy but yet in spiritual poverty. They are kings and priests, yet they still lack the authority to alter the course of nations. Father, I ask You to shake these congregations again; shake them with the power of Your love until they flow from the church into their cities like a mighty river, as You did on the day of Pentecost. Let the earthquake of boldness run through the places where they are assembled until they run with zeal into the marketplace with signs and wonders closely following. Let Your perfect love drive out the fear of man.

"Father, forgive Your prophets for not sounding the trumpet in Zion, calling a solemn assembly, and gathering the warriors to Your holy mountain. Father, forgive them for prophesying for hire and making the gospel of no effect. Father, forgive them for their lack of understanding and compassion and for putting a price tag on Your word. Father, forgive them for not heeding Your call to harvest when they first heard the trumpet, thus losing millions of souls to hell. Forgive them for gathering the people to themselves and leaving behind a generation in the dust of their self-promotion. Father, forgive them for they know not what they do.

"Father, forgive Your evangelists for exchanging the attire of the simple and pure for the fancy and expensive, inevitably distancing themselves from the world they were sent to win. Forgive them for ignoring Your word, '[Having] no form or comeliness [royal, kingly pomp], that we should look at Him, and no beauty that we should desire Him' (Isa. 53:2, AMP). Forgive them, Father, for losing the zeal that once compelled them into the darkest places to shine Your light, exchanging it instead for novel applause. Father, forgive them. Convict them once again. Provoke them to good works and to love.

"Father, forgive a world that has ignored You and grown calloused to Your persistent pleas to repent even in the aftermath of tragedy. Father, forgive the leaders who have promised change but have continued on their course of envy and strife, building their temples of self-gratification. Father, forgive Your Church for not demonstrating love and mercy toward one another, only widening the margin of My return from Heaven to earth. Father, I beseech Thee! Forgive them! Father, raise up an army from the ashes of this contemporary compromise of religion and give them a broken heart. Father, touch their lips with a coal from the altar until they cry with unrestrained passion, *'Here am I, send me!'* "

CHAPTER 30

THE GOSPEL
ACCORDING TO JESUS

Great multitudes followed Jesus as He traveled to Jerusalem. The masses pressed to touch Him and perchance receive something from Him. They tore the roof where He sat and taught. They cried out from the roadsides, "Jesus, Son of David!" The crowds swelled when He broke the bread and blessed the fishes and fed them. They flocked to His side as He healed their children and cast out demons. But in the midst of the fanfare and tumult, Jesus saw the condition of their hearts and motives of their souls. He turned to the multitudes that followed Him and said: "If any man come to me, and hate not his father, and mother, and wife, and children, and brethren, and sisters, yes, and his own life also, he cannot be My disciple. And whosoever doth not bear his cross, and come after Me, cannot be My disciple" (Luke 14:26-27, KJV).

Jesus quickly separated the wheat from the chaff, the sheep from the goats. He knew that some followed Him only for personal gain and purpose. His requirements went beyond superficial sacrifice. His doctrine was one of lose to gain, die to live, serve to be great, and follow to lead. This went against the theology of the day. Theirs was to lord and to loot, to overpower by the strength of the law alone. They demanded usury and obedience by fear instead of love. Church had evolved into a marketplace instead of a safe place. You may not leave with your livelihood!

Jesus' words shattered their presumption and pride. He shocked the masses and offended the religious. He contradicted everything that was comfortable and amiable. He crossed every sacred line and stepped on every holy ground. He refused to please the crowd. His was a message of death and resurrection; something they didn't want to hear. He met every excuse with a challenge, every religious chide with truth. To the zealous follower faced with the reality of His message and what it would cost him, Jesus said, "Let the dead bury their own dead, but you go and preach the kingdom of God" (Luke 9:60). To the one who cared for house and home more than the cross, He said, "No man, having put his hand to the plough, and looking back is fit for the kingdom of God" (Luke 9:62). It was the gospel according to Jesus.

"For the message of the cross is foolishness to them who are perishing" (1 Cor. 1:18). The message of the cross was the power to save, but it was also the power to crush every self-motive and self-ambition into dust. It wasn't just a message of glory, but one of guts. It demanded all of a man or woman. It left nothing to chance; it was all or nothing.

The cross was the price tag of discipleship, the reward for a life less pleasurable, and the only means to revival. To the Jews, it was a stumbling block, and to the Greeks it was foolishness. To the Pharisee and the religious it was a threat that eventually meant death to the one who published it. But to their utter horror, their plotting led only to the cross, which led only to His glory! His message wasn't one of hopelessness! It was one of absolute victory! Its road of suffering led one through the portal of eternity to embrace immortality! It was the gospel according to Jesus.

Yet the modern-day clerical cant is one of no suffering, no sacrifice, no blood, no cross. It is a cross-less Calvary that some preach today—void of its power, conviction, scars, and thorns. The murderous thief next to Christ recognized this paradox as he exclaimed, "Lord, remember me, when You come into Your Kingdom" (Luke 23:42). He identified with the cross and its ability to save. He comprehended that the blood, which splattered on his body as the Man next to him convulsed and heaved, somehow cleared him of his guilt and crime. He knew that this Man hanging next to him had hidden in His heart the mysteries of the universe, of eternal life and immortality. In His furrowed, bloody brow was the care of the Creator for a lost pitiful soul like him. The thief had taken up his cross as well. Only this time he accepted its price and its demand in exchange for his soul, his eternal existence in paradise. He happily followed.

Today it's torture to motivate the modern-day Christian past the ritual of Wednesday and Sunday, to propel them past ground zero of Sunday school into the streets and "Samarias" of America. We mourn as they did in Acts chapter 8, never shaking off the dust of our systematic theology and becoming a tangible presence in our cities and streets. Our light is hidden under a bushel and the skies are filled with the smoke of its smoldering. Oh God, give us Philips who will rise from the ashes of our religion and invade Samaria with a power greater than the psychics and the witches who foretell a fantasy instead of the truth! Give us people who will take up their cross and follow You! "And the multitudes with one accord heeded the things spoken by Philip, hearing and seeing the miracles which he did" (Acts 8:6).

The world isn't demanding a better gospel; it's just expecting a better demonstration of it! People want to *see* His love, not just hear about it! They want to touch Jesus by touching us, not just receive something in the mail or touch a hand over the television. They want to *touch* flesh and blood. They want to see the tears of compassion in our eyes, not some pious religious disguise. ***They need to see Jesus in you and me!***

The psychics will change their message when they see a greater demonstration of prophecy and power! The soothsayer will bow at the feet of Jesus when her heart is laid bare by the cutting sword of the Word of the Lord! The greedy businessman will confess Christ when he comprehends the riches of glory in Christ Jesus! ***We need to show the world something greater than the temporary tapestries that distract them!*** We need to communicate the gospel according to Jesus:

> *Assuredly, I say to you, there is no one who has left house or brothers or sisters or father or mother or wife or children or lands, for My sake and the gospel's, who shall not receive a hundredfold now in this time—houses and brothers and sisters and mothers and children and lands, with persecutions— and in the age to come, eternal life* (Mark 10:29-30).

The crowds that faced Jesus were given an ultimatum of all or nothing. There was no gray on the canvas of obedience. The gospel message wasn't a retirement plan for the rich, but a rescue plan for the poor. It was the only answer to the leper, the only hope for the sinner. It was the midnight cry to the dying, the light of hope to the shipwrecked and blind. It wasn't a winning ticket for the selfish. It was the lifeline to the drowning, a remedy to the sick and destitute. Jesus never stepped on this side of eternity for the righteous, but to call sinners to repentance.

The qualification for Heaven is found in Matthew 7:21-23:

> *Not everyone who says to Me, "Lord, Lord" shall enter the kingdom of heaven, **but he who does the will of My Father in heaven**. Many will say to Me in that day, "Lord, Lord, have we not prophesied in Your name, cast out demons in Your*

*name, and done many wonders in Your name?" And then I
will declare to them, "I never knew you."*

The sheep and the goats stood before Jesus, but only one
reigned with Him. Only one remained with Him.

The sheep were the ones who had recognized Jesus in the
face of their brother, the least of them, the weakest of them. The
only difference between the sheep and the goats was what they
did and didn't do. Now is our only chance to reach out to the
lost! We have all of eternity for revelation, but we have only one
lifetime for salvation! We have all of eternity to discover the mysteries and depths of creation; we have only one life that "is even
a vapor that appears for a little time and then vanishes away"
(James 4:14) to reach out and change a generation from its
course of destruction to deliverance. It's now or never.

"Then Jesus, looking at him, loved him, and said to him,
'One thing you lack: Go your way, sell whatever you have and
give to the poor, and you will have treasure in heaven; and come,
take up the cross, and follow Me' " (Mark 10:21). This is the
gospel according to Jesus. Let's go then! Let's pray the prayer of
faith as they did so long ago. Pray it now: "I hear the voice of the
Lord saying, 'Whom shall we send? Who will go for us?' Then
said I, 'Here am I send me!' " Pray it now! Go to Him and only
Him and pour out your heart like water! He will hear you and
empower you to be His disciple and witness! As in Acts 1:8, He
will give you the power to be His witness! Pray that prayer right
now! "Lord, make me a disciple! Make me a revivalist, that wherever I go, revival surely follows!"

Today is your day to burn with His fire and His desire. I pray
that these words are only a brand plucked from the holy altar in
Heaven and placed on your lips:

Loose them, Lord, and let them boldly declare Your
love and power! Create in them a clean heart and right
spirit; restore to them the joy of their salvation and
burn in them, Lord, with an all-consuming fire. I pray

that the modern prophets of our day, who I believe to be the best equipped and enlightened in history, will take up their plowshares and swords and lead us into battle.

We have become a spiritual consumer rather than a minister. We hoard our manna until the entire camp stinks. We need to give freely what we have received freely, and, as leaders, we need to lead the charge into the streets of our cities. We cannot afford to do anything else. A severe accountability is going to be upon the prophets and ministers of our time. Can you imagine how many conferences and meetings occurred in New York City in 2001? How we can look back now and say to ourselves, "Why didn't I tell someone about Jesus?" Yes, there will be casualties in war, but the numbers that are perishing as the parade of conferences rolls through our cities is staggering. We have to wake up from our religious stupor and run to a dying world. We have to do it now. Let's run to the battle.

For more information on

Additional copies of this book and other
book titles from DESTINY IMAGE are
available at your local bookstore.

For a complete list of our titles,
visit us at www.destinyimage.com
Send a request for a catalog to:

Destiny Image® Publishers, Inc.
P.O. Box 310
Shippensburg, PA 17257-0310

*"Speaking to the Purposes of God for This
Generation and for the Generations to Come"*